50 Island Flavor Recipes for Home

By: Kelly Johnson

Table of Contents

- Tropical Mango Salsa
- Jamaican Jerk Chicken
- Caribbean Conch Fritters
- Hawaiian Poke Bowl
- Bahamian Conch Salad
- Cuban Black Beans and Rice
- Key Lime Pie
- Puerto Rican Mofongo
- Barbadian Flying Fish Cou-Cou
- Trinidadian Doubles
- Maldivian Fish Curry
- Seychellois Octopus Salad
- Mauritian Chicken Daube
- Fijian Kokoda (Marinated Fish)
- Samoan Panipopo (Coconut Buns)
- Tahitian Poisson Cru (Raw Fish Salad)
- Maori Hangi (Traditional Earth Oven Cooked Feast)
- New Caledonian Bougna (Traditional Dish)
- Antiguan Pepperpot
- St. Lucian Green Fig and Saltfish
- Grenadian Oil Down
- Bajan Cou-Cou and Flying Fish
- Mauritian Dholl Puri (Split Pea Pancakes)
- Bahamian Conch Chowder
- Cuban Ropa Vieja
- Hawaiian Loco Moco
- Jamaican Escovitch Fish
- Puerto Rican Arroz con Gandules
- Dominican Mangu
- Maldivian Garudhiya (Fish Soup)
- Seychellois Kat-kat Banane (Banana Dessert)
- Fijian Kokoda (Marinated Fish)
- Samoan Sapasui (Chop Suey)
- Tahitian Po'e (Banana Pudding)
- Maori Rewena Bread

- New Caledonian Boulette (Fish Balls)
- Antiguan Fungi (Cornmeal Dish)
- St. Lucian Breadfruit and Saltfish
- Grenadian Callaloo Soup
- Bajan Fish Cakes
- Mauritian Gateau Piment (Chili Cakes)
- Bahamian Johnnycakes
- Cuban Tostones (Fried Plantains)
- Hawaiian Haupia (Coconut Pudding)
- Jamaican Ackee and Saltfish
- Puerto Rican Pastelón (Plantain Lasagna)
- Dominican Sancocho
- Maldivian Hedhikaa (Short Eats)
- Seychellois Ladob (Banana Dessert)
- Fijian Rourou (Taro Leaves in Coconut Cream)

Tropical Mango Salsa

Ingredients:

- 2 ripe mangoes, diced
- 1 small red onion, finely chopped
- 1 red bell pepper, diced
- 1 jalapeño pepper, seeded and finely chopped
- 1/4 cup fresh cilantro, chopped
- Juice of 1 lime
- Salt and pepper to taste

Instructions:

1. In a medium-sized bowl, combine the diced mangoes, red onion, red bell pepper, jalapeño pepper, and cilantro.
2. Squeeze the lime juice over the mixture and gently toss to combine.
3. Season the salsa with salt and pepper to taste.
4. Cover the bowl with plastic wrap and refrigerate for at least 30 minutes to allow the flavors to meld together.
5. Serve the Tropical Mango Salsa chilled as a topping for grilled fish or chicken, or enjoy it with tortilla chips as a refreshing appetizer. Enjoy!

Jamaican Jerk Chicken

Ingredients:

- 4 chicken breasts or 8 chicken thighs, bone-in and skin-on
- 6 green onions, chopped
- 4 cloves garlic, minced
- 2 Scotch bonnet peppers (or habanero peppers), minced (adjust to taste for spiciness)
- 2 tablespoons fresh thyme leaves
- 2 tablespoons fresh ginger, grated
- 2 tablespoons soy sauce
- 2 tablespoons olive oil
- 2 tablespoons brown sugar
- 2 tablespoons lime juice
- 1 tablespoon ground allspice
- 1 teaspoon ground cinnamon
- 1 teaspoon ground nutmeg
- 1 teaspoon ground black pepper
- 1 teaspoon salt

Instructions:

1. Prepare the Marinade:
    - In a blender or food processor, combine green onions, garlic, Scotch bonnet peppers, thyme, ginger, soy sauce, olive oil, brown sugar, lime juice, allspice, cinnamon, nutmeg, black pepper, and salt. Blend until smooth.
2. Marinate the Chicken:
    - Place chicken pieces in a large bowl or resealable plastic bag.
    - Pour the marinade over the chicken, making sure it's evenly coated.
    - Cover the bowl or seal the bag and refrigerate for at least 4 hours, or ideally overnight, to allow the flavors to penetrate the chicken.
3. Grill the Chicken:
    - Preheat your grill to medium-high heat.
    - Remove the chicken from the marinade, shaking off any excess.
    - Grill the chicken for about 6-8 minutes per side, or until fully cooked through and juices run clear. The internal temperature should reach 165°F (75°C).
4. Serve:

- Once cooked, remove the chicken from the grill and let it rest for a few minutes.
- Serve hot with your favorite side dishes like rice and peas, fried plantains, or Jamaican festivals (sweet fried dumplings).

Enjoy your flavorful Jamaican Jerk Chicken! Adjust the spice level according to your preference, and don't forget to pair it with some cooling sides to balance out the heat.

Caribbean Conch Fritters

Ingredients:

- 1 pound conch meat, finely chopped (you can substitute with shrimp if conch is not available)
- 1 cup all-purpose flour
- 1 teaspoon baking powder
- 1 small onion, finely chopped
- 1 bell pepper, finely chopped
- 2 cloves garlic, minced
- 2 green onions, finely chopped
- 1 Scotch bonnet pepper (or habanero pepper), finely chopped (adjust to taste)
- 1 tablespoon fresh thyme leaves, chopped
- 2 tablespoons fresh parsley, chopped
- 2 eggs, beaten
- 1/4 cup milk
- Salt and black pepper to taste
- Oil for frying

Instructions:

1. Prepare the Conch:
    - If using fresh conch, clean and finely chop it. If using frozen conch, thaw it according to package instructions, then finely chop.
    - Place the chopped conch in a bowl and set aside.
2. Mix the Batter:
    - In a large mixing bowl, combine the flour, baking powder, chopped onion, bell pepper, garlic, green onions, Scotch bonnet pepper, thyme, parsley, salt, and black pepper.
    - Add the beaten eggs and milk to the dry ingredients and mix until well combined.
    - Fold in the chopped conch meat until evenly distributed throughout the batter.
3. Fry the Fritters:
    - Heat oil in a deep fryer or a heavy-bottomed pot to 350°F (175°C).
    - Using a spoon or scoop, carefully drop spoonfuls of the batter into the hot oil, making sure not to overcrowd the pot.

- Fry the fritters for 3-4 minutes, or until they are golden brown and cooked through.
- Remove the fritters from the oil using a slotted spoon and place them on a plate lined with paper towels to drain excess oil.

4. Serve:
   - Serve the conch fritters hot, accompanied by a dipping sauce of your choice, such as a spicy aioli, tartar sauce, or mango salsa.
   - Garnish with fresh parsley or sliced scallions if desired.

Enjoy your Caribbean Conch Fritters as a tasty appetizer or snack, perfect for any occasion with friends and family!

Hawaiian Poke Bowl

Ingredients:

For the Poke:

- 1 pound sushi-grade ahi tuna (or salmon), cubed
- 1/4 cup soy sauce
- 1 tablespoon sesame oil
- 1 tablespoon rice vinegar
- 1 teaspoon grated ginger
- 1 teaspoon honey
- 2 green onions, thinly sliced
- 1 teaspoon sesame seeds
- Optional: 1 teaspoon Sriracha or chili flakes for spice

For the Bowl:

- 2 cups cooked sushi rice or brown rice
- 1 avocado, sliced
- 1 cucumber, thinly sliced or diced
- 1/2 cup shredded carrots
- 1/2 cup edamame, shelled
- 1/4 cup sliced radishes
- 1/4 cup seaweed salad
- Optional toppings: sliced jalapeños, tobiko (flying fish roe), furikake seasoning

Instructions:

1. Prepare the Poke:
   - In a bowl, whisk together soy sauce, sesame oil, rice vinegar, grated ginger, and honey until well combined.
   - Add the cubed tuna (or salmon) to the marinade and gently toss to coat. Allow it to marinate in the refrigerator for at least 15-20 minutes.
2. Assemble the Bowl:
   - Divide the cooked rice among serving bowls.
   - Arrange the marinated tuna (or salmon) on top of the rice.
   - Add the sliced avocado, cucumber, shredded carrots, edamame, sliced radishes, and seaweed salad around the tuna.

3. Finish and Garnish:
    - Drizzle any remaining marinade over the poke bowl for extra flavor.
    - Sprinkle sliced green onions and sesame seeds over the bowls.
    - Add optional toppings such as sliced jalapeños, tobiko, or furikake seasoning for additional flavor and texture.
4. Serve:
    - Serve the Hawaiian Poke Bowls immediately, and enjoy them fresh!

Feel free to customize your Poke Bowl with your favorite ingredients and toppings. You can also adjust the marinade according to your taste preferences, adding more or less of the ingredients listed. Enjoy your delicious taste of Hawaii!

Bahamian Conch Salad

Ingredients:

- 1 pound fresh conch meat, cleaned and diced into small pieces
- 2-3 tomatoes, diced
- 1 onion, finely chopped
- 1 bell pepper (green or red), diced
- 1 cucumber, diced
- 2-3 stalks of celery, finely chopped
- 1-2 Scotch bonnet peppers (or habanero peppers), finely chopped (adjust to taste for spiciness)
- 1 cup fresh cilantro or parsley, chopped
- Juice of 4-6 limes
- Juice of 1-2 oranges
- Salt and freshly ground black pepper to taste
- Optional: diced avocado for garnish

Instructions:

1. Prepare the Conch:
    - If using fresh conch, clean and tenderize it by pounding it with a meat mallet or rolling pin until it's tender. Then, dice it into small pieces.
    - If using frozen conch, thaw it according to package instructions and then dice it into small pieces.
2. Marinate the Conch:
    - In a large mixing bowl, combine the diced conch meat with the juice of the limes and oranges. Make sure the conch is completely submerged in the citrus juices. Let it marinate for about 30 minutes to 1 hour in the refrigerator. The acidity of the citrus juices helps to "cook" the conch, similar to ceviche.
3. Prepare the Vegetables:
    - While the conch is marinating, prepare the vegetables by dicing the tomatoes, onion, bell pepper, cucumber, celery, and Scotch bonnet peppers.
    - Chop the cilantro or parsley finely.
4. Mix Everything Together:
    - After the conch has marinated, drain off most of the excess citrus juice.

- Add the diced vegetables and chopped cilantro or parsley to the bowl with the marinated conch.
- Season with salt and freshly ground black pepper to taste.
- Gently toss everything together until well combined.

5. Chill and Serve:
    - Cover the bowl with plastic wrap and let the Bahamian Conch Salad chill in the refrigerator for about 15-30 minutes to allow the flavors to meld together.
    - Before serving, taste and adjust the seasoning if necessary.
    - Optionally, garnish the salad with diced avocado just before serving.
6. Serve:
    - Serve the Bahamian Conch Salad chilled, as a refreshing appetizer or light meal, ideally enjoyed on a hot summer day.

Enjoy the vibrant flavors of this Bahamian specialty, which perfectly captures the essence of the Caribbean!

Cuban Black Beans and Rice

Ingredients:

For the Black Beans:

- 2 cups dried black beans, soaked overnight (or canned black beans, drained and rinsed)
- 1 onion, finely chopped
- 1 green bell pepper, finely chopped
- 4 cloves garlic, minced
- 2 bay leaves
- 1 teaspoon ground cumin
- 1 teaspoon dried oregano
- 1/2 teaspoon smoked paprika
- Salt and pepper to taste
- 4 cups vegetable or chicken broth (or water)
- 2 tablespoons olive oil

For the Rice:

- 2 cups long-grain white rice
- 4 cups water
- 1 tablespoon olive oil
- Salt to taste

Instructions:

For the Black Beans:

1. Prepare the Beans:
    - If using dried black beans, soak them in water overnight. Drain and rinse before cooking.
    - If using canned black beans, drain and rinse them thoroughly.
2. Cook the Aromatics:
    - Heat olive oil in a large pot over medium heat. Add the chopped onion, bell pepper, and garlic. Sauté until softened, about 5 minutes.
3. Cook the Beans:

- Add the soaked (or canned) black beans to the pot with the sautéed aromatics.
- Stir in the bay leaves, ground cumin, dried oregano, smoked paprika, salt, and pepper.
- Pour in the vegetable or chicken broth (or water) until the beans are fully submerged.

4. Simmer:
   - Bring the mixture to a boil, then reduce the heat to low. Cover the pot and simmer gently for about 1 to 1 1/2 hours, or until the beans are tender and creamy. If using canned beans, simmer for about 30 minutes to allow the flavors to meld.
5. Adjust Seasoning:
   - Taste the beans and adjust the seasoning if needed. Add more salt, pepper, or spices to taste.

For the Rice:

1. Rinse the Rice:
   - Rinse the rice under cold water until the water runs clear. This helps remove excess starch.
2. Cook the Rice:
   - In a separate pot, bring 4 cups of water to a boil. Add a pinch of salt and olive oil.
   - Stir in the rinsed rice and return to a boil. Reduce the heat to low, cover, and simmer for 18-20 minutes, or until the rice is tender and the water is absorbed.
3. Fluff the Rice:
   - Once the rice is cooked, remove it from the heat and let it sit, covered, for a few minutes. Then, fluff the rice with a fork to separate the grains.

Serve:

- Serve the black beans alongside the cooked rice. You can mix the beans and rice together or serve them separately, allowing each person to mix to their liking.
- Garnish with chopped fresh cilantro or parsley, if desired.
- Enjoy your Cuban Black Beans and Rice as a flavorful and satisfying meal!

Feel free to adjust the seasoning and spice levels according to your taste preferences.

This dish is perfect for a comforting and nutritious meal any day of the week!

Key Lime Pie

Ingredients:

For the Crust:

- 1 1/2 cups graham cracker crumbs (about 10-12 graham crackers)
- 1/4 cup granulated sugar
- 6 tablespoons unsalted butter, melted

For the Filling:

- 1 can (14 ounces) sweetened condensed milk
- 4 large egg yolks
- 1/2 cup key lime juice (freshly squeezed if possible)
- Zest of 2 limes

For the Topping (optional):

- 1 cup heavy cream
- 2 tablespoons powdered sugar
- Lime slices or zest for garnish

Instructions:

For the Crust:

1. Preheat the Oven:
    - Preheat your oven to 350°F (175°C).
2. Prepare the Crust:
    - In a mixing bowl, combine the graham cracker crumbs and granulated sugar.
    - Stir in the melted butter until the mixture resembles wet sand and holds together when pressed.
3. Press into Pie Pan:
    - Press the mixture firmly and evenly into the bottom and up the sides of a 9-inch pie pan, forming the crust.
4. Bake the Crust:
    - Bake the crust in the preheated oven for 10 minutes, or until lightly golden brown.

- Remove from the oven and let it cool while you prepare the filling.

For the Filling:

1. Prepare the Filling:
   - In a mixing bowl, whisk together the sweetened condensed milk, egg yolks, key lime juice, and lime zest until smooth and well combined.
2. Pour into Crust:
   - Pour the filling into the cooled graham cracker crust, spreading it evenly.
3. Bake the Pie:
   - Return the pie to the oven and bake for 15-20 minutes, or until the filling is set but still slightly jiggly in the center.
4. Chill:
   - Once baked, remove the pie from the oven and let it cool to room temperature.
   - Then, refrigerate the pie for at least 2 hours, or until thoroughly chilled and set.

For the Topping (Optional):

1. Whip the Cream:
   - In a mixing bowl, whip the heavy cream and powdered sugar until stiff peaks form.
2. Top the Pie:
   - Spread the whipped cream over the chilled pie.
3. Garnish:
   - Garnish the pie with lime slices or zest for a decorative touch.

Serve:

- Slice the Key Lime Pie and serve chilled.
- Enjoy the creamy, tangy goodness of this classic dessert!

Feel free to adjust the sweetness or tartness of the filling to suit your taste preferences. This Key Lime Pie is perfect for any occasion, whether it's a summer barbecue or a special holiday gathering.

Puerto Rican Mofongo

Ingredients:

- 4 green plantains, peeled and sliced into 1-inch pieces
- 4 cloves garlic, minced
- 1 cup pork cracklings (chicharrones), crushed
- 1/4 cup olive oil
- Salt and pepper to taste
- Optional toppings: cooked shrimp, chicken, steak, or pork; garlic butter sauce; tomato sauce; or mojo sauce (a traditional Puerto Rican sauce made with garlic, olive oil, and citrus juice)

Instructions:

1. Fry the Plantains:
    - Heat about 1 inch of oil in a large skillet over medium-high heat.
    - Fry the plantain pieces in batches until golden brown and tender, about 3-4 minutes per side.
    - Remove the fried plantains from the oil and drain them on paper towels.
2. Prepare the Mofongo:
    - In a large mortar and pestle or a sturdy bowl, add the fried plantain pieces and garlic.
    - Use the pestle or a masher to mash the plantains and garlic together until they form a smooth mixture. You can also use a food processor if you don't have a mortar and pestle.
    - Gradually add the crushed pork cracklings and olive oil to the mashed plantains, mixing well after each addition.
    - Season the mofongo with salt and pepper to taste, and continue to mix until everything is well combined.
3. Shape and Serve:
    - To serve, you can shape the mofongo into balls or patties using a mold or simply scoop it onto plates.
    - If desired, top the mofongo with cooked shrimp, chicken, steak, or pork, and drizzle with garlic butter sauce, tomato sauce, or mojo sauce.

Tips:

- Adjust the amount of garlic and pork cracklings to suit your taste preferences.
- You can also customize your mofongo by adding additional ingredients such as cooked bacon, cheese, or herbs.
- Mofongo is often served alongside rice and beans, salad, or fried plantain chips (tostones).

Enjoy the rich flavors and comforting textures of this traditional Puerto Rican dish!

Barbadian Flying Fish Cou-Cou

Ingredients:

For the Cou-Cou:

- 1 cup fine cornmeal (preferably yellow cornmeal)
- 2 cups water
- 1 cup okra, sliced (fresh or frozen)
- 1 onion, finely chopped
- 2 cloves garlic, minced
- 2 cups fish or vegetable broth
- 1 tablespoon butter or margarine
- Salt and pepper to taste

For the Flying Fish Stew:

- 4-6 flying fish fillets (substitute with another type of fish if flying fish is not available)
- 1 onion, sliced
- 2 tomatoes, diced
- 1 bell pepper, sliced
- 2 cloves garlic, minced
- 1 tablespoon tomato paste
- 1 cup fish or vegetable broth
- 2 tablespoons vegetable oil
- Salt and pepper to taste
- Fresh thyme leaves for garnish (optional)

Instructions:

For the Cou-Cou:

1. Prepare the Okra:
    - Trim the ends of the okra and slice them into rounds. Set aside.
2. Prepare the Cornmeal Mixture:
    - In a bowl, mix the cornmeal with 1 cup of water until smooth and lump-free.
3. Cook the Cou-Cou:

- In a saucepan, bring the remaining 1 cup of water to a boil.
- Gradually pour the cornmeal mixture into the boiling water, stirring continuously to prevent lumps from forming.
- Add the sliced okra, chopped onion, minced garlic, and fish or vegetable broth to the pot.
- Reduce the heat to low and simmer, stirring frequently, until the cou-cou thickens and becomes smooth and creamy, about 15-20 minutes.
- Stir in the butter or margarine and season with salt and pepper to taste.

For the Flying Fish Stew:

1. Prepare the Flying Fish:
    - Rinse the flying fish fillets and pat them dry with paper towels. Season with salt and pepper on both sides.
2. Cook the Stew:
    - Heat vegetable oil in a large skillet over medium heat.
    - Add the sliced onion, diced tomatoes, sliced bell pepper, and minced garlic to the skillet. Cook until the vegetables are softened, about 5-7 minutes.
    - Stir in the tomato paste and fish or vegetable broth, and bring the mixture to a simmer.
    - Gently add the seasoned flying fish fillets to the skillet and simmer until the fish is cooked through and flakes easily with a fork, about 5-7 minutes.

Serve:

- To serve, spoon a generous portion of the flying fish stew over the warm cou-cou.
- Garnish with fresh thyme leaves if desired.
- Enjoy your delicious Barbadian Flying Fish Cou-Cou!

This dish is a wonderful representation of Barbadian cuisine and is sure to delight your taste buds with its vibrant flavors and comforting textures.

Trinidadian Doubles

Ingredients:

For the Bara (Fried Bread):

- 2 cups all-purpose flour
- 1 teaspoon baking powder
- 1 teaspoon ground turmeric
- 1 teaspoon ground cumin
- 1/2 teaspoon salt
- 1/2 teaspoon sugar
- 1 cup warm water
- Oil for frying

For the Channa (Chickpea Curry):

- 2 cups cooked chickpeas (canned or cooked from dry)
- 1 onion, finely chopped
- 2 cloves garlic, minced
- 1 tablespoon curry powder
- 1 teaspoon ground cumin
- 1 teaspoon ground turmeric
- 1/2 teaspoon ground coriander
- 1/4 teaspoon cayenne pepper (adjust to taste)
- 1 cup vegetable broth or water
- Salt to taste
- Chopped cilantro for garnish (optional)

For Serving:

- Tamarind chutney
- Mango chutney
- Hot pepper sauce (like Trinidadian pepper sauce or Scotch bonnet pepper sauce)
- Shredded cabbage or lettuce
- Thinly sliced cucumber
- Chopped tomatoes
- Finely chopped onions
- Finely chopped cilantro
- Lime wedges

Instructions:

For the Bara (Fried Bread):

1. Prepare the Dough:
   - In a large mixing bowl, combine the flour, baking powder, turmeric, cumin, salt, and sugar.
   - Gradually add the warm water to the dry ingredients, mixing until a soft dough forms.
   - Knead the dough for a few minutes until smooth and elastic. Cover and let it rest for 30 minutes.
2. Shape and Fry the Bara:
   - Divide the dough into small balls, about the size of golf balls.
   - Flatten each ball into a round, flat disc, about 4-5 inches in diameter.
   - Heat oil in a deep frying pan or skillet over medium-high heat.
   - Fry the bara in batches until golden brown and cooked through, about 2-3 minutes per side. Drain on paper towels.

For the Channa (Chickpea Curry):

1. Prepare the Curry:
   - Heat oil in a large skillet or saucepan over medium heat.
   - Add the chopped onion and garlic, and sauté until softened and translucent, about 2-3 minutes.
   - Stir in the curry powder, cumin, turmeric, coriander, and cayenne pepper, and cook for another minute until fragrant.
   - Add the cooked chickpeas and vegetable broth or water to the skillet. Bring to a simmer and cook for 10-15 minutes, stirring occasionally, until the sauce thickens slightly.
   - Season with salt to taste. If desired, garnish with chopped cilantro before serving.

Assemble the Doubles:

1. Fill the Bara:
   - To assemble, place a spoonful of the channa (chickpea curry) onto one bara.
   - Top with another bara to form a "double."

2. Add Toppings:
    - Drizzle with tamarind chutney, mango chutney, and hot pepper sauce according to your taste preferences.
    - Add shredded cabbage or lettuce, thinly sliced cucumber, chopped tomatoes, onions, and cilantro.
    - Serve with lime wedges on the side.

Enjoy your Trinidadian Doubles as a delicious and satisfying street food snack or meal!

Maldivian Fish Curry

Ingredients:

- 500g firm white fish fillets (such as snapper, grouper, or mahi-mahi), cut into chunks
- 2 tablespoons vegetable oil
- 1 onion, finely chopped
- 2 cloves garlic, minced
- 1-inch piece of ginger, minced
- 2 green chilies, sliced (adjust to taste)
- 1 teaspoon ground turmeric
- 1 teaspoon ground cumin
- 1 teaspoon ground coriander
- 1/2 teaspoon chili powder (adjust to taste)
- 1 can (400ml) coconut milk
- 2 tomatoes, chopped
- 1 tablespoon tamarind paste (or substitute with lime juice)
- Salt to taste
- Fresh cilantro leaves for garnish

Instructions:

1. Prepare the Fish:
   - Rinse the fish fillets under cold water and pat them dry with paper towels. Cut them into bite-sized chunks and set aside.
2. Make the Curry Base:
   - Heat vegetable oil in a large skillet or pot over medium heat.
   - Add the chopped onion, minced garlic, minced ginger, and sliced green chilies. Sauté until the onions are soft and translucent, about 5 minutes.
3. Add Spices:
   - Stir in the ground turmeric, ground cumin, ground coriander, and chili powder. Cook for another minute until fragrant.
4. Cook the Curry:
   - Pour in the coconut milk and stir well to combine with the onion and spice mixture.
   - Add the chopped tomatoes and tamarind paste (or lime juice) to the curry. Stir to combine.
   - Season with salt to taste.

5. Simmer and Add Fish:
   - Bring the curry to a simmer and let it cook for 5-7 minutes to allow the flavors to meld together.
   - Gently add the fish chunks to the curry, making sure they are submerged in the sauce.
   - Cover the skillet or pot and let the fish simmer in the curry for 8-10 minutes, or until the fish is cooked through and flakes easily with a fork.
6. Garnish and Serve:
   - Once the fish is cooked, remove the skillet or pot from the heat.
   - Garnish the Maldivian Fish Curry with fresh cilantro leaves.
   - Serve the curry hot with steamed rice or Maldivian flatbread (roshi) for a delicious and satisfying meal.

Enjoy the rich and aromatic flavors of this Maldivian specialty, perfect for a cozy dinner at home or a gathering with friends and family!

Seychellois Octopus Salad

Ingredients:

For the Octopus:

- 1 large octopus (about 1-1.5 kg), cleaned and prepared
- 1 onion, quartered
- 2 bay leaves
- 2 garlic cloves, crushed
- 1 lemon, halved
- Salt and pepper to taste

For the Salad:

- Cooked octopus (from the above preparation)
- 1 onion, thinly sliced
- 1 cucumber, diced
- 2 tomatoes, diced
- 1 bell pepper (red or green), diced
- 1-2 chili peppers (optional), thinly sliced
- Handful of fresh parsley or cilantro, chopped
- Juice of 1-2 lemons
- 2 tablespoons olive oil
- Salt and pepper to taste

Instructions:

Cooking the Octopus:

1. Prepare the Octopus:
    - Rinse the octopus under cold water and remove any remaining innards.
    - Remove the beak from the center of the tentacles if it's still present.
    - If the octopus is large, you can tenderize it by freezing it for a few hours and then thawing it before cooking.
2. Boil the Octopus:
    - In a large pot of water, add the quartered onion, bay leaves, crushed garlic cloves, lemon halves, salt, and pepper.
    - Bring the water to a boil over high heat.

- Carefully add the octopus to the boiling water.
- Reduce the heat to low and let the octopus simmer gently for about 1-1.5 hours, or until tender. The cooking time will depend on the size of the octopus. You'll know it's done when you can easily insert a fork into the thickest part of the tentacles.

3. Cool and Slice:
   - Once cooked, remove the octopus from the pot and let it cool.
   - Once cooled, slice the octopus into bite-sized pieces. Discard any excess parts like the head or beak.

Assembling the Salad:

1. Prepare the Vinaigrette:
   - In a small bowl, whisk together the lemon juice, olive oil, salt, and pepper to make the vinaigrette.
2. Assemble the Salad:
   - In a large mixing bowl, combine the sliced octopus with the thinly sliced onion, diced cucumber, diced tomatoes, diced bell pepper, sliced chili peppers (if using), and chopped parsley or cilantro.
   - Pour the vinaigrette over the salad ingredients and toss gently to coat everything evenly.
3. Chill and Serve:
   - Cover the bowl and refrigerate the salad for at least 30 minutes to allow the flavors to meld together.
   - Serve the Seychellois Octopus Salad chilled, as a refreshing appetizer or light meal.

Enjoy the vibrant flavors and tender texture of this Seychellois delicacy, perfect for a taste of the islands at home!

Mauritian Chicken Daube

Ingredients:

- 1 whole chicken, cut into pieces (or use bone-in chicken thighs or drumsticks)
- 2 tablespoons vegetable oil
- 2 onions, finely chopped
- 4 cloves garlic, minced
- 1-inch piece of ginger, minced
- 2 tomatoes, chopped
- 2 tablespoons tomato paste
- 1 tablespoon curry powder
- 1 teaspoon ground turmeric
- 1 teaspoon ground coriander
- 1 teaspoon ground cumin
- 1 cinnamon stick
- 2-3 cloves
- 2-3 cardamom pods
- 1 bay leaf
- 2-3 potatoes, peeled and cubed
- 1 carrot, peeled and diced
- 1 cup chicken broth or water
- Salt and pepper to taste
- Fresh cilantro or parsley for garnish

Instructions:

1. Prepare the Chicken:
    - Rinse the chicken pieces under cold water and pat them dry with paper towels. Season with salt and pepper.
2. Brown the Chicken:
    - Heat vegetable oil in a large pot or Dutch oven over medium heat.
    - Brown the chicken pieces in batches until golden brown on all sides. Remove and set aside.
3. Make the Sauce:
    - In the same pot, add the chopped onions and sauté until softened and translucent, about 5 minutes.
    - Add the minced garlic and ginger, and cook for another 1-2 minutes until fragrant.

- Stir in the chopped tomatoes and tomato paste, and cook for a few minutes until the tomatoes break down and release their juices.
4. Add Spices:
    - Add the curry powder, ground turmeric, ground coriander, ground cumin, cinnamon stick, cloves, cardamom pods, and bay leaf to the pot. Stir well to combine and toast the spices for a minute or two.
5. Simmer the Stew:
    - Return the browned chicken pieces to the pot, along with any accumulated juices.
    - Add the cubed potatoes and diced carrot to the pot.
    - Pour in the chicken broth or water, enough to cover the chicken and vegetables.
    - Season with salt and pepper to taste.
6. Cook the Daube:
    - Bring the mixture to a simmer, then reduce the heat to low.
    - Cover the pot and let the daube simmer gently for about 45 minutes to 1 hour, or until the chicken is tender and the sauce has thickened.
7. Garnish and Serve:
    - Once the chicken is cooked through and the sauce has thickened, remove the pot from the heat.
    - Discard the cinnamon stick, cloves, cardamom pods, and bay leaf.
    - Garnish the Mauritian Chicken Daube with fresh cilantro or parsley before serving.

Enjoy your Mauritian Chicken Daube with rice, bread, or roti for a hearty and comforting meal that's bursting with flavor!

Fijian Kokoda (Marinated Fish)

Ingredients:

- 500g fresh fish fillets (such as mahi-mahi, snapper, or mackerel), skinless and boneless, diced into bite-sized pieces
- 1 cup coconut cream (fresh or canned)
- Juice of 4-5 limes or lemons
- 1 small red onion, thinly sliced
- 1-2 chili peppers (such as bird's eye chili or jalapeño), thinly sliced (optional)
- 1 ripe tomato, diced
- 1 cucumber, peeled and diced
- 1 bell pepper (red or green), diced
- Handful of fresh cilantro or parsley, chopped
- Salt and pepper to taste

Instructions:

1. Prepare the Fish:
    - Rinse the fish fillets under cold water and pat them dry with paper towels.
    - Cut the fish into bite-sized pieces and place them in a shallow dish or bowl.
2. Marinate the Fish:
    - Pour the lime or lemon juice over the fish pieces, making sure they are fully submerged.
    - Cover the dish and let the fish marinate in the citrus juice in the refrigerator for about 30 minutes to 1 hour. The acidity of the juice will "cook" the fish, similar to ceviche.
3. Prepare the Vegetables:
    - While the fish is marinating, prepare the vegetables.
    - Thinly slice the red onion and chili peppers (if using).
    - Dice the tomato, cucumber, and bell pepper into small pieces.
    - Chop the fresh cilantro or parsley.
4. Assemble the Kokoda:
    - Once the fish is marinated, drain off most of the citrus juice.
    - In a large mixing bowl, combine the marinated fish with the sliced red onion, diced tomato, cucumber, bell pepper, and chopped cilantro or parsley.
    - Pour the coconut cream over the fish and vegetables.

- Season with salt and pepper to taste.
5. Mix Well and Chill:
    - Gently toss all the ingredients together until well combined.
    - Cover the bowl and refrigerate the Kokoda for at least 1 hour to allow the flavors to meld together and the fish to chill.
6. Serve:
    - Once chilled, give the Kokoda a final stir and taste for seasoning.
    - Serve the Fijian Kokoda chilled, garnished with extra cilantro or parsley if desired.
    - Enjoy as a refreshing and flavorful appetizer or light meal!

Note:

- You can adjust the amount of chili peppers according to your desired level of spiciness.
- Fijian Kokoda is traditionally served in small bowls or dishes, often accompanied by crispy crackers or bread for scooping up the delicious marinated fish and vegetables.

Samoan Panipopo (Coconut Buns)

Ingredients:

For the Buns:

- 4 cups all-purpose flour
- 1/2 cup granulated sugar
- 2 teaspoons active dry yeast
- 1 cup coconut milk (canned or fresh), warmed
- 1/4 cup warm water
- 1/4 cup melted butter or coconut oil
- 1 teaspoon salt
- 1 egg, beaten (for egg wash)

For the Coconut Caramel Sauce:

- 1 can (400ml) coconut milk
- 1/2 cup brown sugar
- 1 teaspoon vanilla extract

Instructions:

For the Buns:

1. Activate the Yeast:
    - In a small bowl, combine the warm water and a pinch of sugar. Sprinkle the active dry yeast over the water and let it sit for about 5-10 minutes until foamy.
2. Make the Dough:
    - In a large mixing bowl, combine the flour, sugar, and salt.
    - Pour the warmed coconut milk and melted butter or coconut oil into the bowl, along with the activated yeast mixture.
    - Mix until a dough forms.
3. Knead the Dough:
    - Transfer the dough to a lightly floured surface and knead for about 8-10 minutes until smooth and elastic. You can also use a stand mixer with a dough hook attachment for this step.
4. First Rise:

- Place the dough in a greased bowl, cover with a clean kitchen towel or plastic wrap, and let it rise in a warm place for about 1-2 hours, or until doubled in size.

5. Shape the Buns:
    - Punch down the risen dough and divide it into equal-sized portions (about 12-16 pieces).
    - Shape each portion into a smooth ball and place them on a lined baking sheet, leaving some space between each bun.
6. Second Rise:
    - Cover the shaped buns with a clean kitchen towel or plastic wrap and let them rise again for about 30-45 minutes, or until puffy.
7. Preheat the Oven:
    - Meanwhile, preheat your oven to 350°F (175°C).
8. Brush with Egg Wash:
    - Once the buns have risen, brush the tops with beaten egg for a shiny finish.
9. Bake the Buns:
    - Bake the buns in the preheated oven for 20-25 minutes, or until golden brown and cooked through.
    - Remove from the oven and let them cool slightly on a wire rack.

For the Coconut Caramel Sauce:

1. Prepare the Sauce:
    - In a saucepan, combine the coconut milk and brown sugar.
    - Bring the mixture to a simmer over medium heat, stirring occasionally until the sugar has dissolved.
2. Simmer:
    - Reduce the heat to low and let the sauce simmer gently for about 10-15 minutes, or until it thickens slightly.
3. Add Vanilla:
    - Stir in the vanilla extract and remove the saucepan from the heat.

Assemble the Panipopo:

1. Top with Sauce:

- Once the buns have cooled slightly, use a fork or skewer to poke holes all over the tops of the buns.
- Pour the warm coconut caramel sauce over the buns, allowing it to seep into the holes and coat the tops.

2. Serve:
    - Let the Panipopo cool for a few minutes before serving.
    - Enjoy these delicious Samoan Coconut Buns warm or at room temperature as a delightful treat!

Note:

- You can adjust the sweetness of the coconut caramel sauce according to your preference by adding more or less brown sugar.
- These Panipopo are best served fresh on the day they are made, but you can store any leftovers in an airtight container at room temperature for up to 2 days. Warm them briefly in the microwave before serving, if desired.

Tahitian Poisson Cru (Raw Fish Salad)

Ingredients:

- 500g fresh fish fillets (such as tuna, mahi-mahi, or snapper), skinless and boneless, diced into bite-sized pieces
- 1 cup coconut milk (canned or fresh)
- Juice of 4-5 limes or lemons
- 1 small red onion, thinly sliced
- 2 tomatoes, diced
- 1 cucumber, peeled and diced
- 1 bell pepper (red or green), diced
- 1-2 chili peppers (such as bird's eye chili or jalapeño), thinly sliced (optional)
- Handful of fresh cilantro or parsley, chopped
- Salt and pepper to taste

Instructions:

1. Prepare the Fish:
    - Rinse the fish fillets under cold water and pat them dry with paper towels.
    - Cut the fish into bite-sized pieces and place them in a shallow dish or bowl.
2. Marinate the Fish:
    - Pour the lime or lemon juice over the fish pieces, making sure they are fully submerged.
    - Cover the dish and let the fish marinate in the citrus juice in the refrigerator for about 30 minutes to 1 hour. The acidity of the juice will "cook" the fish, similar to ceviche.
3. Prepare the Vegetables:
    - While the fish is marinating, prepare the vegetables.
    - Thinly slice the red onion and chili peppers (if using).
    - Dice the tomatoes, cucumber, and bell pepper into small pieces.
    - Chop the fresh cilantro or parsley.
4. Assemble the Poisson Cru:
    - Once the fish is marinated, drain off most of the citrus juice.
    - In a large mixing bowl, combine the marinated fish with the sliced red onion, diced tomatoes, diced cucumber, diced bell pepper, sliced chili peppers (if using), and chopped cilantro or parsley.
    - Pour the coconut milk over the fish and vegetables.

- Season with salt and pepper to taste.
5. Mix Well and Chill:
    - Gently toss all the ingredients together until well combined.
    - Cover the bowl and refrigerate the Poisson Cru for at least 1 hour to allow the flavors to meld together and the fish to chill.
6. Serve:
    - Once chilled, give the Poisson Cru a final stir and taste for seasoning.
    - Serve the Tahitian Poisson Cru chilled, garnished with extra cilantro or parsley if desired.
    - Enjoy as a refreshing and flavorful appetizer or light meal!

Notes:

- You can adjust the amount of chili peppers according to your desired level of spiciness.
- Tahitian Poisson Cru is traditionally served in small bowls or dishes, often accompanied by crispy crackers or breadfruit chips for scooping up the delicious marinated fish and vegetables.

Maori Hangi (Traditional Earth Oven Cooked Feast)

Ingredients:

For the Meat and Protein:

- 1-2 kg of lamb, beef, chicken, or pork (cut into large pieces)
- 500g of fish fillets (optional)
- 500g of shellfish (such as mussels or clams, optional)

For the Vegetables:

- 4-6 large potatoes (peeled and halved)
- 4-6 large kumara (sweet potatoes, peeled and halved)
- 4-6 carrots (peeled and halved)
- 4-6 onions (peeled and halved)
- 4-6 ears of corn (husks removed and halved)
- Other seasonal vegetables of your choice (such as pumpkin, cabbage, or parsnips)

For the Hangi Pit:

- Large heavy-duty aluminum foil
- Large banana leaves or cabbage leaves
- Large clean stones (such as volcanic rocks or river stones)
- Shovel for digging the pit

Instructions:

Preparing the Hangi Pit:

1. Choose a Location:
    - Find a suitable outdoor area for your Hangi pit. Ensure it's away from any flammable materials and has enough space for digging and cooking.
2. Digging the Pit:
    - Dig a pit in the ground, approximately 1 meter deep and wide enough to fit all your food. You can use a shovel or spade for this task.
3. Heating the Stones:

- Place a layer of large, clean stones at the bottom of the pit. Make a fire on top of the stones and let it burn until the stones are very hot, usually about 1-2 hours.

Preparing the Food:

1. Wrap the Food:
   - Season the meat, fish, and shellfish with salt, pepper, and any desired spices or herbs.
   - Wrap each type of protein and vegetable separately in large banana leaves or cabbage leaves, then wrap again in heavy-duty aluminum foil.
2. Layering the Food:
   - Once the stones are hot, carefully remove any large flames and embers from the pit.
   - Layer the wrapped food on top of the hot stones, starting with the meat and fish at the bottom, followed by the root vegetables, and finally the corn and other vegetables on top.
3. Covering the Pit:
   - Cover the food with more banana leaves or cabbage leaves to keep the moisture in, then cover the pit with a thick layer of soil to seal in the heat.

Cooking the Hangi:

1. Cooking Time:
   - Let the food cook in the pit for 2-4 hours, depending on the size and type of food. The longer it cooks, the more tender and flavorful it will be.
2. Checking for Doneness:
   - After the cooking time has elapsed, carefully uncover the pit and remove the foil packages of food.
   - Check for doneness by inserting a fork or knife into the meat and vegetables. They should be tender and cooked through.
3. Serving the Hangi:
   - Carefully unwrap the foil packages and transfer the cooked food to serving platters.
   - Serve the Maori Hangi feast hot, with traditional accompaniments such as Maori bread (rewana) and condiments like salt and watercress.

Enjoy your Maori Hangi feast, a delicious and unique culinary experience that celebrates the traditional cooking methods of the Maori people of New Zealand!

New Caledonian Bougna (Traditional Dish)

Ingredients:

For the Bougna:

- 500g chicken thighs or fish fillets (cut into pieces)
- 2-3 large taro roots (peeled and sliced)
- 2-3 large sweet potatoes (peeled and sliced)
- 2-3 plantains (peeled and sliced)
- 2 onions (sliced)
- 2 tomatoes (sliced)
- 2-3 carrots (peeled and sliced)
- 2-3 green bell peppers (sliced)
- Salt and pepper to taste
- Coconut milk (optional)
- Banana leaves or aluminum foil

For the Underground Oven (Traditional Method):

- Large banana leaves or aluminum foil
- Shovel for digging the pit
- Large clean stones or bricks
- Firewood or charcoal

Instructions:

Preparing the Bougna:

1. Season the Meat or Fish:
    - Season the chicken thighs or fish fillets with salt and pepper to taste. You can also marinate them in coconut milk for extra flavor if desired.
2. Layering the Ingredients:
    - On a large piece of banana leaf or aluminum foil, layer the sliced taro roots, sweet potatoes, plantains, onions, tomatoes, carrots, and bell peppers.
    - Place the seasoned meat or fish on top of the vegetables.
3. Wrapping the Bougna:

- Fold the banana leaf or aluminum foil over the ingredients to form a tight packet, ensuring that the Bougna is well sealed.

Cooking the Bougna:

1. Preparing the Underground Oven:
   - If using the traditional method, dig a pit in the ground and line it with large clean stones or bricks.
   - Build a fire on top of the stones and let it burn until the stones are very hot, usually about 1-2 hours.
2. Layering the Bougna in the Pit:
   - Once the stones are hot, carefully remove any large flames and embers from the pit.
   - Place the wrapped Bougna packets on top of the hot stones, ensuring they are evenly distributed.
3. Covering and Cooking:
   - Cover the Bougna packets with more banana leaves or aluminum foil to seal in the moisture and flavor.
   - Cover the pit with a thick layer of soil to trap the heat and steam.
   - Let the Bougna cook in the underground oven for 1-2 hours, depending on the size and thickness of the ingredients.
4. Checking for Doneness:
   - After the cooking time has elapsed, carefully uncover the pit and remove the Bougna packets.
   - Open one packet to check if the meat or fish is cooked through and the vegetables are tender. If not, return the packets to the pit and cook for additional time.
5. Serving the Bougna:
   - Carefully unwrap the Bougna packets and transfer the cooked ingredients to serving plates or bowls.
   - Serve the Bougna hot, with traditional accompaniments such as rice or bread.

Enjoy your New Caledonian Bougna, a delicious and wholesome dish that celebrates the rich culinary traditions of the Pacific!

Antiguan Pepperpot

Ingredients:

- 500g stewing beef, cut into chunks
- 500g pork ribs or pork shoulder, cut into chunks
- 500g chicken pieces (with bone-in), such as thighs or drumsticks
- 1 cup salted pigtail or salted beef (optional), soaked and rinsed
- 1 cup okra, trimmed and sliced
- 2 cups spinach or callaloo leaves, chopped
- 2 cups pumpkin or squash, diced
- 2 cups sweet potato, diced
- 2 cups yam or dasheen (taro root), diced
- 2 cups eggplant, diced
- 2 cups cassava or yuca, peeled and diced
- 2 cups coconut milk
- 2 onions, chopped
- 4 cloves garlic, minced
- 2-3 Scotch bonnet peppers, whole (adjust to taste)
- 4-6 sprigs thyme
- 4-6 whole cloves
- 4-6 whole allspice berries
- Salt and pepper to taste
- Water or beef broth, as needed
- Oil for frying

Instructions:

1. Prepare the Meat:
    - If using salted pigtail or salted beef, soak it in water overnight to remove excess salt. Rinse well before using.
    - Season the beef, pork, and chicken pieces with salt and pepper.
2. Brown the Meat:
    - Heat oil in a large pot or Dutch oven over medium-high heat.
    - Brown the seasoned meat in batches until golden brown on all sides. Remove and set aside.
3. Saute Aromatics:
    - In the same pot, sauté the chopped onions and minced garlic until softened and fragrant.

4. Combine Meat and Aromatics:
    - Return the browned meat to the pot with the onions and garlic.
5. Add Seasonings:
    - Tie the thyme sprigs, whole cloves, and whole allspice berries in a cheesecloth bundle or secure them in a spice bag. Add the bundle to the pot.
    - Add the whole Scotch bonnet peppers to the pot. Be careful not to burst them, as they are very spicy. You can remove them later if desired.
6. Add Vegetables and Liquid:
    - Add the diced pumpkin, sweet potato, yam, eggplant, cassava, and any other root vegetables you're using to the pot.
    - Pour in enough water or beef broth to cover the meat and vegetables.
    - Bring the mixture to a boil, then reduce the heat to low and let it simmer for about 1-2 hours, or until the meat is tender and the vegetables are cooked through.
7. Add Coconut Milk:
    - Stir in the coconut milk and let the Pepperpot simmer for an additional 10-15 minutes, allowing the flavors to meld together.
8. Add Okra and Greens:
    - Add the sliced okra and chopped spinach or callaloo leaves to the pot.
    - Let the Pepperpot simmer for another 10 minutes, or until the okra is tender and the greens are wilted.
9. Adjust Seasoning:
    - Taste the Pepperpot and adjust the seasoning with salt and pepper as needed.
10. Serve:
    - Remove the Scotch bonnet peppers and spice bundle from the pot before serving.
    - Serve the Antiguan Pepperpot hot, accompanied by rice, bread, or dumplings for a delicious and satisfying meal.

Enjoy your Antiguan Pepperpot, a comforting and flavorful dish that's perfect for sharing with family and friends!

St. Lucian Green Fig and Saltfish

Ingredients:

- 500g saltfish (salted codfish)
- 4-6 green bananas (green figs)
- 2 tablespoons vegetable oil
- 1 onion, finely chopped
- 2 cloves garlic, minced
- 1 bell pepper, chopped
- 2 tomatoes, chopped
- 2-3 sprigs thyme
- 2-3 scallions, chopped
- 2-3 wiri wiri peppers or Scotch bonnet peppers, finely chopped (optional)
- Salt and black pepper to taste
- Fresh parsley or cilantro for garnish (optional)

Instructions:

1. Prepare the Saltfish:
    - Rinse the saltfish under cold water to remove excess salt. Place it in a large bowl and cover with water. Let it soak for at least 4 hours or overnight, changing the water a few times.
2. Boil the Green Bananas:
    - Peel the green bananas and cut them into chunks.
    - Place the banana chunks in a pot of boiling water and cook for about 15-20 minutes, or until tender when pierced with a fork. Drain and set aside.
3. Prepare the Saltfish:
    - Once the saltfish has soaked, drain it and rinse it under cold water again.
    - Flake the saltfish into small pieces, removing any bones and skin.
4. Cook the Saltfish:
    - Heat the vegetable oil in a large skillet or frying pan over medium heat.
    - Add the chopped onion, minced garlic, and chopped bell pepper to the skillet. Sauté until the vegetables are softened and fragrant, about 3-4 minutes.
5. Add Tomatoes and Seasonings:

- Add the chopped tomatoes, thyme sprigs, chopped scallions, and chopped wiri wiri peppers or Scotch bonnet peppers (if using) to the skillet. Cook for another 2-3 minutes.
6. Add Saltfish:
    - Add the flaked saltfish to the skillet, stirring to combine with the vegetables and seasonings. Cook for an additional 5-7 minutes, allowing the flavors to meld together.
7. Add Green Bananas:
    - Add the cooked green banana chunks to the skillet with the saltfish mixture. Gently toss everything together until well combined.
8. Season and Garnish:
    - Season the Green Fig and Saltfish with salt and black pepper to taste. Adjust seasoning as needed.
    - Garnish with fresh parsley or cilantro if desired.
9. Serve:
    - Serve the St. Lucian Green Fig and Saltfish hot, as a hearty and flavorful meal on its own, or with bread, rice, or boiled provisions.

Enjoy this delicious taste of St. Lucia!

Grenadian Oil Down

Ingredients:

- 500g chicken pieces (bone-in)
- 500g salted pork or bacon, diced
- 2 cups coconut milk
- 2 cups water or chicken broth
- 2 cups pumpkin, diced
- 2 cups breadfruit, diced
- 2 cups cassava or yuca, peeled and diced
- 2 cups sweet potato, peeled and diced
- 2 cups green beans, trimmed and halved
- 2 cups spinach or callaloo leaves, chopped
- 2 onions, chopped
- 4 cloves garlic, minced
- 2-3 wiri wiri peppers or Scotch bonnet peppers, whole or chopped (adjust to taste)
- 4-6 sprigs thyme
- 4-6 whole cloves
- 4-6 whole allspice berries
- Salt and black pepper to taste
- Vegetable oil for frying

Instructions:

1. Prepare the Ingredients:
    - Rinse the chicken pieces under cold water and pat them dry with paper towels. Season them with salt and pepper.
    - If using salted pork or bacon, soak it in water for about 1 hour to remove excess salt. Rinse and drain before using.
    - Peel and dice the pumpkin, breadfruit, cassava, sweet potato, and any other root vegetables you're using. Trim and halve the green beans. Chop the onions, garlic, and wiri wiri peppers.
2. Heat Oil and Brown Meat:
    - Heat a couple of tablespoons of vegetable oil in a large pot or Dutch oven over medium-high heat.
    - Brown the seasoned chicken pieces and diced salted pork or bacon in the hot oil until golden brown on all sides. Remove and set aside.

3. Layer Ingredients:
   - In the same pot, layer the diced vegetables, starting with the heartier ones like pumpkin, breadfruit, cassava, and sweet potato. Add the green beans and spinach or callaloo leaves on top.
4. Add Aromatics and Seasonings:
   - Scatter the chopped onions, minced garlic, and chopped wiri wiri peppers or Scotch bonnet peppers over the vegetables.
   - Tie the thyme sprigs, whole cloves, and whole allspice berries in a cheesecloth bundle or secure them in a spice bag. Add the bundle to the pot.
5. Add Coconut Milk and Water:
   - Pour the coconut milk and water (or chicken broth) over the layered vegetables and seasonings.
6. Cook the Oil Down:
   - Bring the mixture to a boil, then reduce the heat to low and let it simmer, covered, for about 1-2 hours, or until the vegetables are tender and the liquid has been absorbed.
7. Check for Doneness:
   - Check the Oil Down occasionally and add more liquid if needed to prevent it from sticking to the bottom of the pot. The dish is done when the vegetables are soft and the liquid has been absorbed.
8. Serve:
   - Remove the spice bundle and discard.
   - Serve the Grenadian Oil Down hot, as a delicious and satisfying one-pot meal that celebrates the flavors of the Caribbean.

Enjoy your taste of Grenada with this flavorful and comforting dish!

Bajan Cou-Cou and Flying Fish

Ingredients:

For the Cou-Cou:

- 1 cup cornmeal
- 2 cups water
- 1 cup okra, finely chopped
- 1 onion, finely chopped
- 2 cloves garlic, minced
- 2 cups vegetable or chicken broth
- Salt and pepper to taste
- Butter or margarine (optional)

For the Flying Fish:

- 4-6 fresh flying fish fillets (substitute with another white fish if unavailable)
- Juice of 1-2 limes or lemons
- Salt and pepper to taste
- Flour for dredging
- Vegetable oil for frying

For the Sauce (optional):

- 1 onion, finely chopped
- 2 tomatoes, chopped
- 1 bell pepper, chopped
- 2 cloves garlic, minced
- 1 cup vegetable or chicken broth
- 1 tablespoon tomato paste
- Salt and pepper to taste
- Hot pepper sauce (optional)

Instructions:

For the Cou-Cou:

1. Prepare the Okra:

- In a small saucepan, bring 1 cup of water to a boil. Add the chopped okra and cook for about 5 minutes until softened. Drain and set aside.

2. Make the Cou-Cou:
    - In a large saucepan, bring the remaining 2 cups of water to a boil.
    - Gradually whisk in the cornmeal, stirring constantly to prevent lumps from forming.
    - Reduce the heat to low and continue cooking, stirring frequently, until the mixture thickens, about 15-20 minutes.
    - Stir in the cooked okra, chopped onion, minced garlic, and vegetable or chicken broth.
    - Cook, stirring constantly, until the cou-cou is smooth and creamy. Season with salt and pepper to taste.
    - For a richer flavor, stir in a knob of butter or margarine before serving.

For the Flying Fish:

1. Prepare the Fish:
    - Rinse the flying fish fillets under cold water and pat them dry with paper towels.
    - Season the fish fillets with lime or lemon juice, salt, and pepper.
2. Dredge and Fry the Fish:
    - Dredge the seasoned fish fillets in flour, shaking off any excess.
    - Heat vegetable oil in a large skillet over medium heat.
    - Fry the fish fillets in the hot oil until golden brown and crispy on both sides, about 3-4 minutes per side.

For the Sauce (optional):

1. Make the Sauce:
    - In a separate saucepan, heat a little vegetable oil over medium heat.
    - Add the chopped onion, chopped tomatoes, chopped bell pepper, and minced garlic. Cook until the vegetables are softened.
    - Stir in the vegetable or chicken broth and tomato paste. Simmer for a few minutes until the sauce thickens slightly.
    - Season with salt, pepper, and hot pepper sauce to taste.

Serve:

1. Serve the Dish:
    - Spoon a generous portion of cou-cou onto each plate.
    - Top with fried flying fish fillets.
    - Serve with the optional sauce on the side.
    - Enjoy your Bajan Cou-Cou and Flying Fish, a delicious taste of Barbados!

Feel free to customize this dish according to your preferences and enjoy the flavors of the Caribbean!

Mauritian Dholl Puri (Split Pea Pancakes)

Ingredients:

For the Dholl Puri Dough:

- 1 cup yellow split peas (dholl)
- 1 cup all-purpose flour
- 1 teaspoon turmeric powder
- Salt to taste
- Water, as needed

For Filling and Serving (Optional):

- Cooked yellow split peas (from the dough)
- Chutneys (such as coriander chutney or tamarind chutney)
- Pickles (such as mango pickle or lime pickle)
- Chili paste or sauce
- Sliced tomatoes
- Sliced onions
- Fresh coriander leaves

Instructions:

1. Prepare the Dholl Puri Dough:

   1. Soak the Split Peas:
      - Rinse the yellow split peas thoroughly and soak them in water for at least 4 hours or overnight.
   2. Grind the Split Peas:
      - Drain the soaked split peas and transfer them to a blender or food processor.
      - Grind the split peas into a smooth paste, adding a little water if needed to help with the grinding process.
   3. Mix the Dough:
      - In a large mixing bowl, combine the ground split pea paste with all-purpose flour, turmeric powder, and salt.
      - Gradually add water and knead the mixture into a smooth, pliable dough. The dough should be soft and slightly sticky.

4. Rest the Dough:
   - Cover the dough with a clean kitchen towel or plastic wrap and let it rest for about 30 minutes to 1 hour.

2. Prepare and Cook the Dholl Puri:

   1. Divide the Dough:
      - Divide the rested dough into small balls, about the size of a golf ball.
   2. Roll Out the Puri:
      - On a lightly floured surface, flatten each dough ball into a small disc using your hands.
      - Use a rolling pin to roll out each disc into a thin, round flatbread, about 6-8 inches in diameter. Dust with flour as needed to prevent sticking.
   3. Cook the Puri:
      - Heat a non-stick skillet or tawa over medium-high heat.
      - Place one rolled-out puri onto the hot skillet and cook for about 1-2 minutes on each side, or until lightly golden brown and cooked through.
      - Repeat with the remaining dough balls, cooking each puri individually. You can brush a little oil or ghee on the skillet if desired, but it's not necessary.
   4. Keep Warm:
      - As each puri is cooked, transfer it to a plate and cover with a clean kitchen towel to keep warm while you cook the rest.

3. Serve the Dholl Puri:

   1. Serve Warm:
      - Serve the Mauritian Dholl Puri warm, accompanied by cooked yellow split peas (from the dough) and your choice of chutneys, pickles, chili paste, sliced tomatoes, onions, and fresh coriander leaves.
   2. Enjoy:
      - To eat, place a spoonful of cooked split peas in the center of each puri, along with your desired condiments and toppings.
      - Fold or roll the puri around the filling and enjoy it as a delicious and satisfying street food snack or meal.

Note:

- Dholl Puri is best enjoyed fresh and warm. If you have any leftover puris, you can store them in an airtight container at room temperature and reheat them briefly before serving.

Bahamian Conch Chowder

Ingredients:

- 1 lb conch meat, cleaned and diced
- 2 tablespoons vegetable oil
- 1 onion, chopped
- 2 cloves garlic, minced
- 2 carrots, diced
- 2 celery stalks, diced
- 2 potatoes, diced
- 1 red bell pepper, diced
- 1 green bell pepper, diced
- 1 can (14 oz) diced tomatoes
- 4 cups fish or seafood broth
- 1 cup coconut milk
- 2 bay leaves
- 1 teaspoon thyme leaves
- Salt and pepper to taste
- Fresh parsley or cilantro, chopped (for garnish)
- Lime wedges (for serving)

Instructions:

1. Prepare the Conch:
    - If using fresh conch, clean and dice it into small pieces. If using frozen conch, thaw it according to the package instructions.
2. Saute Aromatics:
    - Heat vegetable oil in a large pot or Dutch oven over medium heat.
    - Add chopped onion and minced garlic. Saute until softened and fragrant, about 2-3 minutes.
3. Add Vegetables:
    - Add diced carrots, celery, potatoes, red bell pepper, and green bell pepper to the pot. Cook for another 5 minutes, stirring occasionally.
4. Add Conch and Tomatoes:
    - Add diced conch meat to the pot and cook for 2-3 minutes, stirring frequently.
    - Pour in the diced tomatoes (with their juices) and stir to combine.
5. Simmer:

- Pour fish or seafood broth into the pot, along with coconut milk.
- Add bay leaves and thyme leaves. Season with salt and pepper to taste.
- Bring the chowder to a boil, then reduce the heat to low and let it simmer for about 20-25 minutes, or until the vegetables are tender and the flavors have melded together.

6. Adjust Seasoning:
   - Taste the chowder and adjust the seasoning with salt and pepper if needed.
7. Serve:
   - Ladle the Bahamian Conch Chowder into serving bowls.
   - Garnish with chopped fresh parsley or cilantro.
   - Serve hot with lime wedges on the side for squeezing over the chowder.
8. Enjoy!

Notes:

- You can customize the chowder by adding other seafood such as shrimp or fish fillets.
- Serve the chowder with crusty bread or crackers for dipping.

Cuban Ropa Vieja

Ingredients:

For the Beef:

- 2 lbs flank steak or skirt steak
- 1 onion, chopped
- 4 cloves garlic, minced
- 1 green bell pepper, sliced
- 1 red bell pepper, sliced
- 1 can (14 oz) diced tomatoes
- 1 cup beef broth
- 1 tablespoon tomato paste
- 1 teaspoon ground cumin
- 1 teaspoon paprika
- 1 teaspoon dried oregano
- Salt and pepper to taste
- Vegetable oil for cooking

For Serving:

- Cooked white rice
- Black beans (optional)
- Sliced avocado
- Chopped fresh cilantro or parsley
- Lime wedges

Instructions:

1. Prepare the Beef:
    - Season the flank steak or skirt steak generously with salt and pepper on both sides.
2. Sear the Beef:
    - Heat vegetable oil in a large Dutch oven or deep skillet over medium-high heat.
    - Sear the seasoned steak on both sides until browned, about 3-4 minutes per side. Remove the steak from the pot and set aside.
3. Saute Aromatics:

- In the same pot, add chopped onion and minced garlic. Cook until softened and fragrant, about 2-3 minutes.
- Add sliced green bell pepper and red bell pepper to the pot. Cook for another 2-3 minutes until slightly softened.
4. Add Tomatoes and Spices:
    - Stir in diced tomatoes, beef broth, tomato paste, ground cumin, paprika, and dried oregano. Mix well to combine.
5. Simmer the Sauce:
    - Return the seared steak to the pot, nestling it into the sauce. Bring the mixture to a simmer.
6. Braise the Beef:
    - Reduce the heat to low, cover the pot, and let the beef simmer gently in the sauce for 2-3 hours, or until the meat is very tender and easily shreds with a fork.
7. Shred the Beef:
    - Once the beef is tender, remove it from the pot and transfer it to a cutting board.
    - Use two forks to shred the beef into thin strips, shredding it against the grain for the best texture.
8. Finish the Sauce:
    - Return the shredded beef to the pot and simmer for another 10-15 minutes to allow the flavors to meld together and the sauce to thicken slightly.
    - Taste and adjust the seasoning with salt and pepper if needed.
9. Serve:
    - Serve the Cuban Ropa Vieja hot, spooned over cooked white rice.
    - Garnish with optional black beans, sliced avocado, chopped fresh cilantro or parsley, and lime wedges on the side for squeezing over the dish.
10. Enjoy your flavorful Cuban Ropa Vieja!

Hawaiian Loco Moco

Ingredients:

For the Hamburger Patties:

- 1 lb ground beef
- 1/2 onion, finely chopped
- 2 cloves garlic, minced
- 1 tablespoon Worcestershire sauce
- Salt and pepper to taste
- Vegetable oil for cooking

For the Gravy:

- 2 tablespoons butter
- 2 tablespoons all-purpose flour
- 2 cups beef broth
- 2 tablespoons soy sauce
- Salt and pepper to taste

For Serving:

- Cooked white rice
- Fried eggs (1 per serving)
- Chopped green onions (optional, for garnish)
- Soy sauce or hot sauce (optional, for serving)

Instructions:

1. Prepare the Hamburger Patties:

　1. In a large mixing bowl, combine the ground beef, finely chopped onion, minced garlic, Worcestershire sauce, salt, and pepper.
　2. Use your hands to gently mix the ingredients until well combined, but avoid overmixing to keep the patties tender.
　3. Divide the mixture into equal portions and shape them into hamburger patties, about 1/2 inch thick.
　4. Heat a skillet or frying pan over medium-high heat and add a little vegetable oil.

5. Cook the hamburger patties for 3-4 minutes on each side, or until they are cooked through and browned on the outside. Remove them from the pan and set aside.

2. Make the Gravy:

1. In the same skillet or frying pan used to cook the hamburger patties, melt the butter over medium heat.
2. Sprinkle the flour over the melted butter and whisk continuously to form a roux. Cook the roux for 1-2 minutes, or until it turns golden brown.
3. Gradually whisk in the beef broth and soy sauce, stirring constantly to prevent lumps from forming.
4. Bring the gravy to a simmer and cook for a few minutes until it thickens to your desired consistency.
5. Season the gravy with salt and pepper to taste. If it's too thick, you can add a little more beef broth to thin it out.

3. Assemble the Loco Moco:

1. Place a serving of cooked white rice on each plate.
2. Top the rice with a cooked hamburger patty.
3. Fry an egg sunny-side up or over-easy and place it on top of the hamburger patty.
4. Spoon the brown gravy generously over the entire dish.
5. Garnish with chopped green onions if desired.
6. Serve the Hawaiian Loco Moco hot, with soy sauce or hot sauce on the side for extra flavor.

4. Enjoy your delicious Hawaiian Loco Moco!

Feel free to customize your Loco Moco with additional toppings such as sautéed mushrooms, crispy bacon, or avocado slices according to your preference.

Jamaican Escovitch Fish

Ingredients:

For the Fried Fish:

- 2 lbs whole fish (such as snapper, parrotfish, or kingfish), cleaned and scaled
- 1 cup all-purpose flour
- 1 teaspoon salt
- 1/2 teaspoon black pepper
- Vegetable oil for frying

For the Escovitch Sauce:

- 1 onion, thinly sliced
- 1 carrot, julienned or thinly sliced
- 1 bell pepper (red, green, or yellow), thinly sliced
- 2 Scotch bonnet peppers, thinly sliced (adjust to taste)
- 3 cloves garlic, thinly sliced
- 1 cup white vinegar
- 1/2 cup water
- 2 tablespoons sugar
- 1 teaspoon salt
- 1 teaspoon whole allspice berries
- 2 bay leaves
- 1/2 teaspoon ground turmeric (optional, for color)
- Vegetable oil for sautéing

For Garnish:

- Fresh cilantro or parsley, chopped
- Lime wedges

Instructions:

1. Prepare the Fried Fish:

    1. Rinse the whole fish under cold water and pat dry with paper towels.
    2. In a shallow dish, combine the all-purpose flour, salt, and black pepper.
    3. Dredge the fish in the seasoned flour mixture, shaking off any excess.

4. Heat vegetable oil in a large skillet or frying pan over medium-high heat.
5. Fry the fish in the hot oil until golden brown and cooked through, about 5-7 minutes per side depending on the size of the fish. Remove from the oil and drain on paper towels.

2. Make the Escovitch Sauce:

1. In a separate saucepan, heat a little vegetable oil over medium heat.
2. Add the thinly sliced onion, carrot, bell pepper, Scotch bonnet peppers, and garlic to the saucepan. Sauté for 2-3 minutes until slightly softened but still crisp.
3. In a small bowl, combine the white vinegar, water, sugar, salt, whole allspice berries, bay leaves, and ground turmeric (if using). Stir until the sugar and salt are dissolved.
4. Pour the vinegar mixture over the sautéed vegetables in the saucepan.
5. Bring the mixture to a simmer and cook for 3-5 minutes, stirring occasionally, until the vegetables are tender but still retain their shape.
6. Remove the saucepan from the heat and let the Escovitch sauce cool slightly.

3. Assemble the Escovitch Fish:

1. Place the fried fish on a serving platter.
2. Spoon the Escovitch sauce generously over the top of the fish, covering it completely.
3. Garnish with chopped fresh cilantro or parsley.
4. Serve the Jamaican Escovitch Fish warm, accompanied by lime wedges for squeezing over the fish.

4. Enjoy your flavorful Jamaican Escovitch Fish!

Feel free to adjust the level of spiciness by adding more or fewer Scotch bonnet peppers according to your preference. Serve this dish with Jamaican rice and peas or fried plantains for a complete meal.

Puerto Rican Arroz con Gandules

Ingredients:

- 2 cups long-grain white rice
- 1 can (15 oz) pigeon peas (gandules), drained and rinsed
- 3 cups water or chicken broth
- 1 onion, finely chopped
- 1 bell pepper (green or red), finely chopped
- 3 cloves garlic, minced
- 2 tablespoons tomato sauce or paste
- 2 tablespoons sofrito (store-bought or homemade)
- 1 packet sazón seasoning (optional)
- 2 tablespoons olive oil
- Salt and pepper to taste
- Chopped fresh cilantro or parsley (for garnish)

Instructions:

1. Prepare the Rice:
   - Rinse the rice under cold water until the water runs clear. Drain and set aside.
2. Saute Aromatics:
   - In a large pot or Dutch oven, heat olive oil over medium heat.
   - Add chopped onion and bell pepper to the pot. Saute until softened, about 3-4 minutes.
   - Add minced garlic and saute for another 1-2 minutes until fragrant.
3. Add Tomato Sauce and Sofrito:
   - Stir in tomato sauce or paste and sofrito. Cook for 2-3 minutes to allow the flavors to meld together.
4. Add Rice and Seasonings:
   - Add the rinsed rice to the pot, stirring to coat it with the onion, pepper, and tomato mixture.
   - Season with sazón seasoning (if using), salt, and pepper to taste. Stir well to combine.
5. Add Water and Pigeon Peas:
   - Pour water or chicken broth into the pot, making sure the liquid covers the rice by about 1 inch.

- Add drained and rinsed pigeon peas (gandules) to the pot. Stir gently to distribute them evenly.
6. Simmer the Rice:
    - Bring the mixture to a boil over high heat, then reduce the heat to low.
    - Cover the pot with a tight-fitting lid and let the rice simmer for 20-25 minutes, or until the liquid is absorbed and the rice is tender.
7. Fluff and Serve:
    - Once the rice is cooked, remove the pot from the heat and let it sit, covered, for 5 minutes.
    - Use a fork to fluff the rice gently.
    - Taste and adjust the seasoning if needed.
8. Garnish and Serve:
    - Transfer the Arroz con Gandules to a serving dish.
    - Garnish with chopped fresh cilantro or parsley before serving.
    - Serve the Puerto Rican Arroz con Gandules hot as a side dish or as a main course with your favorite protein, such as roasted pork or chicken.

Enjoy your flavorful and aromatic Puerto Rican Arroz con Gandules!

Dominican Mangu

Ingredients:

- 4 green plantains
- Salt to taste
- Water for boiling
- 1 medium onion, thinly sliced
- 2 tablespoons vegetable oil or butter
- Queso Frito (fried cheese) or salami (optional, for serving)
- Avocado slices (optional, for serving)

Instructions:

1. Prepare the Plantains:
   - Peel the green plantains by slicing off both ends, then scoring the peel lengthwise with a knife and removing it in strips.
   - Cut the peeled plantains into chunks, about 2 inches in length.
2. Boil the Plantains:
   - Place the plantain chunks in a large pot and cover them with water. Add a pinch of salt to the water.
   - Bring the water to a boil over high heat, then reduce the heat to medium-low and simmer the plantains for about 15-20 minutes, or until they are tender and easily pierced with a fork.
3. Make the Mangu:
   - Once the plantains are cooked, drain them and transfer them to a large mixing bowl.
   - Use a potato masher or fork to mash the plantains until smooth and creamy. Add a little water if needed to achieve the desired consistency.
   - Season the mashed plantains with salt to taste.
4. Sauté the Onions:
   - While the plantains are boiling, heat vegetable oil or butter in a skillet over medium heat.
   - Add the thinly sliced onion to the skillet and sauté until softened and lightly caramelized, about 5-7 minutes.
5. Serve:
   - To serve, place a generous portion of mashed plantains (mangu) on a plate.
   - Top the mangu with the sautéed onions.

- Serve the Dominican Mangu hot, accompanied by fried cheese (queso frito), slices of fried salami, and/or avocado slices if desired.

Enjoy your delicious and comforting Dominican Mangu!

Maldivian Garudhiya (Fish Soup)

Ingredients:

- 500g fresh fish (such as tuna), cleaned and cut into chunks
- 1 onion, sliced
- 2-3 garlic cloves, minced
- 2-3 green chilies, sliced (adjust to taste)
- 2-3 curry leaves
- 2-inch piece of ginger, sliced
- 2-3 tomatoes, chopped
- 1 tablespoon fenugreek seeds
- 1 tablespoon cumin seeds
- 1 tablespoon coriander seeds
- 1 tablespoon turmeric powder
- Salt to taste
- Water
- Fresh lime or lemon wedges, for serving
- Cooked rice, for serving

Instructions:

1. Prepare the Fish:
    - Clean the fish thoroughly and cut it into chunks. You can use any type of fresh fish, but tuna is commonly used in Maldivian Garudhiya.
2. Prepare the Spices:
    - In a mortar and pestle, crush the fenugreek seeds, cumin seeds, and coriander seeds to release their flavors.
3. Cook the Soup:
    - In a large pot, heat some water over medium heat.
    - Add the sliced onion, minced garlic, sliced green chilies, curry leaves, sliced ginger, chopped tomatoes, crushed spices, and turmeric powder to the pot.
    - Season with salt to taste.
    - Add more water to cover the ingredients in the pot.
4. Simmer:
    - Bring the soup to a boil, then reduce the heat to low and let it simmer for about 15-20 minutes, allowing the flavors to meld together.
5. Add the Fish:

- Once the soup base is fragrant and flavorful, add the fish chunks to the pot.
- Let the fish cook in the soup for another 5-7 minutes, or until cooked through and tender.

6. Serve:
    - Ladle the hot Garudhiya into bowls.
    - Serve the Maldivian fish soup with cooked rice on the side.
    - Garnish with fresh lime or lemon wedges for squeezing over the soup before eating.

Enjoy your comforting and flavorful Maldivian Garudhiya! Adjust the spice levels and ingredients according to your taste preferences.

Seychellois Kat-kat Banane (Banana Dessert)

Ingredients:

- 4 ripe bananas
- 1 cup coconut milk
- 1/4 cup granulated sugar (adjust to taste)
- 1/2 teaspoon ground cinnamon
- 1/4 teaspoon ground nutmeg
- Pinch of salt
- 1 tablespoon butter (optional)
- 1 teaspoon vanilla extract (optional)
- Freshly grated coconut or toasted coconut flakes (optional, for garnish)

Instructions:

1. Prepare the Bananas:
    - Peel the ripe bananas and slice them into rounds, about 1/2 inch thick.
2. Cook the Bananas:
    - In a skillet or frying pan, combine the coconut milk, granulated sugar, ground cinnamon, ground nutmeg, and a pinch of salt.
    - Heat the mixture over medium heat, stirring occasionally, until the sugar is dissolved and the coconut milk is warm.
    - Add the sliced bananas to the skillet and gently stir to coat them in the coconut milk mixture.
3. Simmer:
    - Allow the bananas to simmer in the coconut milk mixture for 5-7 minutes, or until they are tender and cooked through. Be careful not to overcook them, as they may become mushy.
4. Add Butter and Vanilla (Optional):
    - If desired, stir in a tablespoon of butter and a teaspoon of vanilla extract to enhance the flavor of the dessert. This step is optional but adds richness and depth to the dish.
5. Serve:
    - Once the bananas are cooked to your liking and the sauce has thickened slightly, remove the skillet from the heat.
    - Transfer the Kat-kat Banane to serving bowls.
    - Garnish with freshly grated coconut or toasted coconut flakes for added texture and flavor, if desired.

6. Enjoy your Seychellois Kat-kat Banane!

Tips:

- You can adjust the sweetness of the dessert by adding more or less sugar according to your taste preferences.
- Feel free to customize the dish by adding other spices such as cloves or cardamom for additional flavor.
- Serve the Kat-kat Banane warm as a comforting dessert, or let it cool slightly for a refreshing treat.

Fijian Kokoda (Marinated Fish)

Ingredients:

- 1 lb fresh fish fillets (such as mahi-mahi, snapper, or tuna), skinless and boneless, cut into bite-sized pieces
- 1 cup coconut milk (freshly squeezed or canned)
- Juice of 3-4 limes or lemons
- 1 small onion, finely diced
- 1 small red bell pepper, finely diced
- 1 small green bell pepper, finely diced
- 1 small cucumber, finely diced
- 1-2 ripe tomatoes, diced
- 1-2 green chilies, finely chopped (adjust to taste)
- Handful of fresh cilantro or parsley, chopped
- Salt and pepper to taste
- Optional: 1-2 tablespoons coconut cream (for garnish)
- Optional: Toasted coconut flakes or fried shallots (for garnish)

Instructions:

1. Prepare the Fish:
    - Rinse the fish fillets under cold water and pat them dry with paper towels.
    - Cut the fish into bite-sized pieces and place them in a non-reactive bowl (glass or ceramic).
2. Marinate the Fish:
    - Pour the lime or lemon juice over the fish pieces, making sure they are fully submerged.
    - Cover the bowl and let the fish marinate in the citrus juice in the refrigerator for at least 30 minutes to 1 hour. The acid in the juice will "cook" the fish, turning it opaque and firm.
3. Prepare the Coconut Milk Mixture:
    - In a separate bowl, combine the coconut milk, finely diced onion, diced bell peppers, diced cucumber, diced tomatoes, chopped green chilies, and chopped cilantro or parsley.
    - Season the coconut milk mixture with salt and pepper to taste. Stir well to combine.
4. Assemble the Kokoda:
    - Once the fish has marinated, drain off the excess lime or lemon juice.

- Add the marinated fish to the coconut milk mixture and gently fold everything together until the fish is evenly coated.
5. Chill and Serve:
    - Cover the bowl with plastic wrap and refrigerate the Kokoda for at least 1-2 hours to allow the flavors to meld together and the fish to absorb the coconut milk mixture.
    - Before serving, taste and adjust the seasoning if needed.
    - Optionally, drizzle some coconut cream over the top of the Kokoda for extra richness and garnish with toasted coconut flakes or fried shallots for added texture and flavor.
6. Enjoy your refreshing and flavorful Fijian Kokoda!

Serve the Kokoda chilled as an appetizer or light meal, accompanied by crusty bread or crackers. It's a perfect dish for warm weather or anytime you're craving something light and refreshing.

Samoan Sapasui (Chop Suey)

Ingredients:

- 1 lb beef chuck or chicken thighs, thinly sliced
- 2 tablespoons vegetable oil
- 1 onion, thinly sliced
- 2-3 garlic cloves, minced
- 1-inch piece of ginger, grated
- 2 carrots, thinly sliced
- 1 bell pepper, thinly sliced
- 1 cup sliced cabbage
- 1 cup sliced mushrooms
- 1 cup sliced snow peas or snap peas
- 1 cup sliced celery
- 1 cup bean sprouts (optional)
- 1 can (8 oz) sliced water chestnuts, drained (optional)
- 1 can (8 oz) bamboo shoots, drained (optional)
- 1/4 cup soy sauce
- 2 tablespoons oyster sauce
- 1 tablespoon Worcestershire sauce
- 1 tablespoon brown sugar
- Salt and pepper to taste
- Cooked rice, for serving

Instructions:

1. Prepare the Meat:
    - If using beef chuck, slice it thinly against the grain. If using chicken thighs, remove the skin and bone, then slice the meat thinly.
2. Sear the Meat:
    - Heat vegetable oil in a large skillet or wok over medium-high heat.
    - Add the sliced meat to the skillet and sear until browned on all sides. Remove the meat from the skillet and set aside.
3. Saute Aromatics and Vegetables:
    - In the same skillet, add more oil if needed.
    - Add sliced onion, minced garlic, and grated ginger to the skillet. Saute until fragrant.

- Add sliced carrots, bell pepper, cabbage, mushrooms, snow peas, celery, bean sprouts (if using), water chestnuts (if using), and bamboo shoots (if using) to the skillet. Stir-fry for a few minutes until the vegetables are slightly softened.
4. Make the Sauce:
    - In a small bowl, whisk together soy sauce, oyster sauce, Worcestershire sauce, and brown sugar until well combined.
5. Simmer:
    - Return the seared meat to the skillet with the vegetables.
    - Pour the sauce over the meat and vegetables in the skillet.
    - Stir everything together until evenly coated with the sauce.
    - Reduce the heat to low, cover the skillet, and let the Sapasui simmer for about 10-15 minutes, or until the meat is tender and the vegetables are cooked to your liking.
6. Adjust Seasoning and Serve:
    - Taste the Sapasui and adjust the seasoning with salt and pepper if needed.
    - Serve the Sapasui hot over cooked rice.
7. Enjoy your delicious Samoan Sapasui!

Feel free to customize the Sapasui with your favorite vegetables or protein options. It's a versatile dish that can be adjusted to suit your taste preferences.

Tahitian Po'e (Banana Pudding)

Ingredients:

- 4 ripe bananas, peeled and mashed
- 1 cup tapioca pearls
- 2 cups coconut milk
- 1/2 cup granulated sugar (adjust to taste)
- 1 teaspoon vanilla extract
- 1/4 teaspoon ground cinnamon (optional)
- Pinch of salt
- Banana leaves or parchment paper (for steaming)

Instructions:

1. Prepare the Tapioca Pearls:
   - Rinse the tapioca pearls under cold water until the water runs clear.
   - In a medium saucepan, bring water to a boil. Add the rinsed tapioca pearls and cook according to the package instructions until they are translucent and tender. This usually takes about 10-15 minutes. Stir occasionally to prevent sticking.
   - Once cooked, drain the tapioca pearls and set them aside.
2. Prepare the Banana Mixture:
   - In a large mixing bowl, combine the mashed ripe bananas, coconut milk, granulated sugar, vanilla extract, ground cinnamon (if using), and a pinch of salt. Mix well until the sugar is dissolved and the ingredients are evenly combined.
3. Combine the Banana Mixture and Tapioca Pearls:
   - Add the cooked tapioca pearls to the banana mixture. Stir gently to combine, making sure the tapioca pearls are evenly distributed throughout the mixture.
4. Assemble and Steam the Po'e:
   - Line a steamer basket or a large pot with banana leaves or parchment paper.
   - Pour the banana and tapioca mixture into the lined steamer basket or pot, spreading it out evenly.
   - Cover the steamer basket or pot with a lid.
5. Steam the Po'e:

- Steam the Po'e over medium heat for about 45 minutes to 1 hour, or until set and firm to the touch. The exact steaming time may vary depending on the thickness of the Po'e.
6. Cool and Serve:
    - Once cooked, remove the Po'e from the steamer and let it cool slightly.
    - Cut the Po'e into squares or slices.
    - Serve the Tahitian Po'e warm or chilled, garnished with additional sliced bananas or grated coconut if desired.
7. Enjoy your delicious and creamy Tahitian Po'e!

This dessert is perfect for serving at gatherings or as a sweet treat any time you're craving something tropical and comforting.

Maori Rewena Bread

Ingredients:

For the Rewena Starter:

- 2 cups mashed potatoes (cooled to room temperature)
- 2 cups all-purpose flour
- 1 tablespoon sugar
- 1/4 teaspoon active dry yeast

For the Bread Dough:

- 4 cups all-purpose flour
- 1 teaspoon salt
- 1 tablespoon sugar
- 1 cup warm water
- 1/4 cup melted butter or oil

Instructions:

1. Prepare the Rewena Starter:

   1. In a large mixing bowl, combine the mashed potatoes, all-purpose flour, sugar, and active dry yeast. Mix well to form a thick paste.
   2. Cover the bowl with a clean kitchen towel or plastic wrap and let it sit at room temperature for 2-3 days, stirring once or twice a day. The mixture will start to ferment and develop a slightly sour smell.

2. Make the Bread Dough:

   1. In a separate large mixing bowl, combine the all-purpose flour, salt, and sugar.
   2. Add the warm water and melted butter or oil to the dry ingredients, along with the prepared rewena starter.
   3. Mix everything together until a dough forms. You may need to add a little more flour or water as needed to achieve the right consistency.
   4. Knead the dough on a floured surface for about 10 minutes, or until it is smooth and elastic.

3. Let the Dough Rise:

    1. Place the dough in a lightly greased bowl, cover it with a clean kitchen towel or plastic wrap, and let it rise in a warm place for 1-2 hours, or until doubled in size.

4. Shape and Bake the Bread:

    1. Once the dough has risen, punch it down to release the air bubbles and divide it into two equal portions.
    2. Shape each portion into a round loaf and place them on a lightly greased baking sheet.
    3. Cover the loaves with a clean kitchen towel and let them rise for another 30-45 minutes.

5. Preheat the Oven:

    1. Preheat your oven to 375°F (190°C) while the loaves are rising.

6. Bake the Bread:

    1. Bake the loaves in the preheated oven for 30-40 minutes, or until they are golden brown and sound hollow when tapped on the bottom.
    2. Remove the bread from the oven and let them cool on a wire rack before slicing and serving.

7. Enjoy your homemade Maori Rewena Bread!

This bread is delicious served warm with butter or jam, or as a side to soups and stews.

The unique flavor and texture make it a favorite in Maori cuisine.

New Caledonian Boulette (Fish Balls)

Ingredients:

- 500g fresh fish fillets (such as tuna, mackerel, or snapper), deboned and skinned
- 1 onion, finely chopped
- 2 cloves garlic, minced
- 2 tablespoons chopped fresh parsley
- 1 tablespoon chopped fresh cilantro (coriander)
- 1 teaspoon grated fresh ginger
- 1 teaspoon ground cumin
- 1 teaspoon ground paprika
- Salt and pepper to taste
- 1 egg, beaten
- 2 tablespoons all-purpose flour (optional, for binding)
- Oil for frying

Instructions:

1. Prepare the Fish: Rinse the fish fillets under cold water and pat dry with paper towels. Cut the fish into chunks and place them in a food processor.
2. Make the Mixture: Add the chopped onion, minced garlic, parsley, cilantro, grated ginger, ground cumin, paprika, salt, and pepper to the food processor with the fish. Pulse the mixture until it forms a coarse paste.
3. Form the Balls: Transfer the fish mixture to a bowl. Add the beaten egg and flour (if using), then mix well until everything is combined evenly. Use your hands to form the mixture into small balls, about the size of golf balls.
4. Fry the Boulette: Heat oil in a frying pan over medium heat. Once the oil is hot, carefully place the fish balls into the pan, making sure not to overcrowd them. Fry the boulette in batches if necessary, turning them occasionally, until they are golden brown and cooked through, about 5-7 minutes.
5. Serve: Once cooked, remove the boulette from the pan and drain them on paper towels to remove excess oil. Serve hot with your favorite dipping sauce or alongside rice and vegetables for a complete meal.

Enjoy your New Caledonian Boulette!

Antiguan Fungi (Cornmeal Dish)

Ingredients:

- 1 cup fine cornmeal
- 3 cups water or chicken/vegetable broth
- 1 onion, finely chopped
- 1 bell pepper, finely chopped
- 2 cloves garlic, minced
- 2 tablespoons butter or margarine
- Salt and pepper to taste

Instructions:

1. Prepare the Vegetables: Heat a tablespoon of butter or margarine in a saucepan over medium heat. Add the chopped onion, bell pepper, and minced garlic. Sauté the vegetables until they are soft and translucent, about 5-7 minutes.
2. Boil the Water/Broth: In a separate pot, bring the water or broth to a boil over high heat.
3. Add Cornmeal: Once the water/broth is boiling, gradually add the cornmeal to the pot, stirring continuously with a whisk to prevent lumps from forming. Reduce the heat to low to maintain a gentle simmer.
4. Cook the Cornmeal: Continue to cook the cornmeal, stirring constantly, until it thickens and pulls away from the sides of the pot, about 10-15 minutes. The consistency should be smooth and creamy.
5. Combine with Vegetables: Once the cornmeal is cooked, add the sautéed vegetables to the pot. Stir well to combine, allowing the flavors to meld together.
6. Season: Season the Antiguan Fungi with salt and pepper to taste. Adjust the seasoning according to your preference.
7. Serve: Transfer the Antiguan Fungi to a serving dish. You can serve it hot as a side dish alongside your favorite Caribbean main dishes, such as grilled fish or stewed meats.

Enjoy your taste of Antiguan cuisine with this comforting and flavorful cornmeal dish!

St. Lucian Breadfruit and Saltfish

Ingredients:

- 1 large breadfruit
- 1 pound salted codfish (saltfish)
- 1 onion, finely chopped
- 2 cloves garlic, minced
- 1 bell pepper, diced
- 2 tomatoes, diced
- 2 tablespoons cooking oil
- 1 teaspoon thyme leaves
- 1 teaspoon black pepper
- 1 teaspoon paprika
- Hot pepper (optional), finely chopped
- Salt (if needed, depending on the saltiness of the codfish)
- Chopped parsley or green onions for garnish (optional)

Instructions:

1. Prepare the Saltfish: Rinse the salted codfish under cold water to remove excess salt. Place the fish in a large bowl and cover it with cold water. Let it soak for at least 4 hours or overnight in the refrigerator, changing the water several times to reduce the saltiness. Once soaked, drain the fish and shred it into small pieces.
2. Prepare the Breadfruit: Peel the breadfruit and cut it into quarters. Remove the core and any tough parts, then cut the flesh into bite-sized chunks. Place the breadfruit pieces in a pot of salted water and bring it to a boil. Cook until the breadfruit is tender but still holds its shape, about 15-20 minutes. Drain and set aside.
3. Cook the Saltfish: In a large skillet or frying pan, heat the cooking oil over medium heat. Add the chopped onion, minced garlic, and diced bell pepper. Sauté until the vegetables are softened and fragrant, about 3-5 minutes.
4. Add the Saltfish: Add the shredded salted codfish to the skillet with the sautéed vegetables. Stir well to combine and cook for another 5-7 minutes, allowing the flavors to meld together.
5. Season: Season the saltfish mixture with thyme leaves, black pepper, paprika, and hot pepper (if using). Taste and adjust the seasoning if needed. Be mindful of adding additional salt, as the codfish may still be salty.

6. Combine with Breadfruit: Add the cooked breadfruit pieces and diced tomatoes to the skillet with the saltfish mixture. Gently toss everything together until well combined. Cook for a few more minutes to heat through and allow the flavors to blend.
7. Serve: Transfer the St. Lucian Breadfruit and Saltfish to a serving platter. Garnish with chopped parsley or green onions if desired. Serve hot as a hearty and flavorful main dish.

Enjoy this taste of Saint Lucia with its vibrant flavors and comforting ingredients!

Grenadian Callaloo Soup

Ingredients:

- 1 bunch callaloo leaves (about 1 pound), washed and chopped (substitute spinach or Swiss chard if callaloo is unavailable)
- 1 onion, finely chopped
- 2 cloves garlic, minced
- 2 tomatoes, diced
- 1 carrot, diced
- 1 medium potato, diced
- 1/2 cup diced pumpkin or squash
- 1 cup coconut milk
- 4 cups vegetable or chicken broth
- 1 tablespoon cooking oil
- 1 teaspoon fresh thyme leaves (or 1/2 teaspoon dried thyme)
- 1 teaspoon ground allspice
- Salt and pepper to taste
- Hot pepper (optional), finely chopped for heat
- 1 pound crab meat or salted meat (optional, for added flavor and protein)
- Lime wedges for serving

Instructions:

1. Prepare the Callaloo: If using fresh callaloo leaves, wash them thoroughly and remove any tough stems. Chop the leaves into bite-sized pieces.
2. Sauté Aromatics: Heat the cooking oil in a large pot over medium heat. Add the chopped onion and minced garlic, and sauté until the onions are translucent and fragrant, about 3-5 minutes.
3. Add Vegetables: Add the diced tomatoes, carrot, potato, and pumpkin or squash to the pot. Stir well to combine with the onions and garlic.
4. Cook Soup Base: Pour in the vegetable or chicken broth and coconut milk. Bring the mixture to a simmer and let it cook for about 15-20 minutes, or until the vegetables are tender.
5. Season: Season the soup with fresh thyme leaves, ground allspice, salt, and pepper. Add the hot pepper for additional heat if desired. Taste and adjust the seasoning according to your preference.

6. Add Callaloo (or Spinach/Swiss Chard): Add the chopped callaloo leaves to the pot. If using spinach or Swiss chard, add them at this stage as well. Stir the soup and allow the greens to wilt and cook down, about 5-7 minutes.
7. Optional Protein: If using crab meat or salted meat, add it to the soup and let it simmer for a few more minutes to heat through.
8. Serve: Ladle the Grenadian Callaloo Soup into bowls. Squeeze fresh lime juice over each serving for a burst of acidity. Serve hot and enjoy!

This flavorful and comforting soup is perfect for a cold day or anytime you want a taste of Grenadian cuisine.

Bajan Fish Cakes

Ingredients:

- 1 cup salted codfish (saltfish), soaked and shredded
- 1 cup all-purpose flour
- 1 small onion, finely chopped
- 1/2 cup finely chopped bell pepper (red or green)
- 2 cloves garlic, minced
- 2 tablespoons chopped fresh parsley
- 1 teaspoon baking powder
- 1/2 teaspoon baking soda
- 1/2 teaspoon ground black pepper
- 1/2 teaspoon hot pepper sauce (optional)
- 1/2 cup water (or more as needed)
- Oil for frying

Instructions:

1. Prepare the Salted Codfish: Rinse the salted codfish under cold water to remove excess salt. Place it in a bowl and cover it with cold water. Let it soak for at least 4 hours or overnight in the refrigerator, changing the water several times. Once soaked, drain the codfish and shred it into small pieces.
2. Make the Batter: In a large mixing bowl, combine the shredded codfish, flour, chopped onion, chopped bell pepper, minced garlic, chopped parsley, baking powder, baking soda, black pepper, and hot pepper sauce (if using). Gradually add the water while stirring, until you achieve a thick batter consistency. The batter should hold together but not be too stiff.
3. Fry the Fish Cakes: Heat oil in a frying pan or skillet over medium heat. Drop spoonfuls of the fish cake batter into the hot oil, shaping them into small patties using a spoon or your hands. Fry the fish cakes in batches, making sure not to overcrowd the pan. Cook until golden brown and crispy on both sides, about 3-4 minutes per side.
4. Drain and Serve: Once cooked, remove the fish cakes from the oil and drain them on paper towels to remove excess oil.
5. Serve: Serve the Bajan Fish Cakes hot, either on their own or with your favorite dipping sauce or hot pepper sauce on the side.

Enjoy these delicious Bajan Fish Cakes as a tasty snack or appetizer, bursting with flavor from the saltfish and aromatic seasonings!

Mauritian Gateau Piment (Chili Cakes)

Ingredients:

- 1 cup yellow split peas (dhal)
- 1 onion, finely chopped
- 2-3 green chilies, finely chopped (adjust to taste)
- 2 cloves garlic, minced
- 1-inch piece of ginger, grated
- 2 tablespoons chopped fresh coriander (cilantro)
- 1 teaspoon ground turmeric
- 1 teaspoon ground cumin
- 1 teaspoon ground coriander
- Salt to taste
- Oil for deep-frying

Instructions:

1. Prepare the Yellow Split Peas: Rinse the yellow split peas under cold water, then soak them in water for at least 4 hours or overnight. Drain the soaked split peas before using.
2. Grind the Split Peas: In a food processor or blender, grind the soaked and drained yellow split peas into a coarse paste. You may need to add a little water to help with the grinding process, but be careful not to make it too watery. Transfer the ground split peas to a large mixing bowl.
3. Mix Ingredients: To the ground split peas, add the finely chopped onion, green chilies, minced garlic, grated ginger, chopped fresh coriander, ground turmeric, ground cumin, ground coriander, and salt to taste. Mix everything together until well combined.
4. Form Patties: Take a small amount of the mixture and shape it into small patties or cakes, about 1 1/2 inches in diameter and 1/2 inch thick. You can shape them using your hands or a spoon.
5. Fry the Chili Cakes: Heat oil in a deep frying pan or skillet over medium heat. Once the oil is hot, carefully add the formed patties in batches, making sure not to overcrowd the pan. Fry the chili cakes until they are golden brown and crispy on the outside, about 3-4 minutes per side. Use a slotted spoon to remove them from the oil and drain them on paper towels to remove excess oil.
6. Serve: Mauritian Gateau Piment is best served hot as a snack or appetizer. They can be enjoyed on their own or with a dipping sauce of your choice.

Enjoy the spicy and flavorful Mauritian Gateau Piment as a delightful snack, perfect for any occasion!

Bahamian Johnnycakes

Ingredients:

- 2 cups all-purpose flour
- 1 cup cornmeal
- 1/4 cup granulated sugar
- 1 tablespoon baking powder
- 1 teaspoon salt
- 1/2 cup butter, softened
- 3/4 cup milk (or more if needed)
- Oil for frying (if frying)

Instructions:

1. Prepare the Dough: In a large mixing bowl, combine the all-purpose flour, cornmeal, sugar, baking powder, and salt. Mix well to combine all the dry ingredients.
2. Add Butter: Cut the softened butter into small pieces and add it to the dry ingredients. Using your fingers or a pastry cutter, rub the butter into the flour mixture until it resembles coarse crumbs.
3. Mix in Milk: Gradually add the milk to the flour mixture, stirring continuously, until a soft dough forms. You may need to add a little more milk if the dough is too dry, or a little more flour if it's too wet. The dough should be soft and slightly sticky.
4. Shape the Johnnycakes: Divide the dough into equal portions and shape each portion into a flat, round cake, about 1/2 inch thick.
5. Fry or Bake: You have two options for cooking the Johnnycakes:
    - Frying: Heat oil in a frying pan or skillet over medium heat. Once the oil is hot, carefully add the shaped Johnnycakes to the pan, cooking in batches if necessary. Fry the cakes until golden brown on both sides, about 3-4 minutes per side. Remove from the oil and drain on paper towels.
    - Baking: Preheat your oven to 375°F (190°C). Place the shaped Johnnycakes on a greased baking sheet or parchment paper-lined baking tray. Bake in the preheated oven for 20-25 minutes, or until the cakes are golden brown and cooked through.
6. Serve: Serve the Bahamian Johnnycakes warm, either on their own or with butter, jam, or honey for added flavor. They are perfect for breakfast, brunch, or as a snack any time of the day.

Enjoy these delightful Bahamian Johnnycakes, crispy on the outside and soft on the inside, for a taste of the Caribbean!

Cuban Tostones (Fried Plantains)

Ingredients:

- 2 green (unripe) plantains
- Vegetable oil for frying
- Salt to taste
- Optional: garlic sauce or mojo for dipping

Instructions:

1. Prepare the Plantains: Using a knife, cut off the ends of the plantains and make a lengthwise slit along the ridges of each plantain. Carefully peel away the skin and discard. Cut the peeled plantains into slices, each about 1 inch thick.
2. Fry the Plantains (First Fry): Heat vegetable oil in a frying pan or skillet over medium-high heat. Once the oil is hot, add the plantain slices in batches, making sure not to overcrowd the pan. Fry the plantains for about 2-3 minutes on each side, or until they are lightly golden but still tender. Remove the fried plantains from the oil and transfer them to a paper towel-lined plate to drain excess oil.
3. Flatten the Plantains: Using the back of a flat surface such as a plate or a tostonera (a specialized tool for flattening plantains), flatten each fried plantain slice into a thin disk. You can also use the bottom of a glass or a jar if you don't have a tostonera.
4. Fry Again (Second Fry): Return the flattened plantain slices to the hot oil, frying them in batches as needed. Fry the plantains for another 2-3 minutes on each side, or until they are crispy and golden brown. Remove the tostones from the oil and place them on a paper towel-lined plate to drain excess oil.
5. Season and Serve: While the tostones are still hot, sprinkle them with salt to taste. Serve the Cuban tostones warm as a side dish or snack, either on their own or with a dipping sauce such as garlic sauce or mojo.

Enjoy these crispy and flavorful Cuban tostones as a delicious addition to your meal or as a tasty snack any time of the day!

Hawaiian Haupia (Coconut Pudding)

Ingredients:

- 1 can (13.5 oz) coconut milk
- 1 cup water
- 1/2 cup sugar
- 1/2 cup cornstarch
- Optional: toasted coconut flakes for garnish

Instructions:

1. Mix Ingredients: In a saucepan, whisk together the coconut milk, water, sugar, and cornstarch until well combined and smooth.
2. Cook Mixture: Place the saucepan over medium heat and bring the mixture to a gentle boil, stirring constantly to prevent lumps from forming.
3. Simmer: Once the mixture reaches a boil, reduce the heat to low and continue to simmer, stirring constantly, until the mixture thickens to a pudding-like consistency. This usually takes about 5-7 minutes.
4. Pour into Mold: Pour the thickened haupia mixture into a shallow dish or mold. You can use individual serving dishes or a single large dish, depending on your preference.
5. Chill: Allow the haupia to cool to room temperature, then cover it with plastic wrap and refrigerate for at least 2-3 hours, or until set.
6. Serve: Once the haupia is set, cut it into squares or rectangles if using a large dish, or simply scoop it out if using individual dishes. Garnish with toasted coconut flakes if desired.
7. Enjoy: Serve the Hawaiian Haupia chilled as a refreshing and creamy coconut dessert.

This Hawaiian Haupia recipe is easy to make and yields a deliciously smooth and creamy pudding with a delightful coconut flavor. It's a perfect treat to enjoy on a warm day or at any special occasion!

Jamaican Ackee and Saltfish

Ingredients:

- 1 can (19 oz) ackee, drained and rinsed
- 8 oz salted codfish (saltfish), soaked and flaked
- 1 onion, chopped
- 1 bell pepper (green or red), chopped
- 2 tomatoes, chopped
- 2 cloves garlic, minced
- 2-3 scallions, chopped
- 1-2 Scotch bonnet peppers or habanero peppers, seeded and finely chopped (optional)
- 2 tablespoons cooking oil
- 1 teaspoon ground black pepper
- Salt (if needed, depending on the saltiness of the codfish)
- Fresh thyme leaves, for garnish (optional)

Instructions:

1. Prepare the Saltfish: Rinse the salted codfish under cold water to remove excess salt. Place it in a bowl and cover it with cold water. Let it soak for at least 4 hours or overnight in the refrigerator, changing the water several times. Once soaked, drain the codfish and flake it into small pieces.
2. Cook the Saltfish: In a large skillet or frying pan, heat the cooking oil over medium heat. Add the chopped onion, bell pepper, and minced garlic. Sauté until the vegetables are softened and fragrant, about 3-5 minutes.
3. Add the Flaked Saltfish: Add the flaked saltfish to the skillet with the sautéed vegetables. Stir well to combine and cook for another 5-7 minutes, allowing the flavors to meld together.
4. Add Tomatoes and Scallions: Add the chopped tomatoes and scallions to the skillet. Stir well and cook for a few more minutes until the tomatoes start to soften.
5. Incorporate Ackee: Gently fold in the drained and rinsed ackee into the skillet with the saltfish and vegetables. Be careful not to break up the ackee too much. Cook for an additional 2-3 minutes, stirring gently to heat through.
6. Season: Season the Jamaican Ackee and Saltfish with ground black pepper. Taste and adjust the seasoning if needed. Be mindful of adding additional salt, as the codfish may still be salty.

7. Serve: Transfer the Jamaican Ackee and Saltfish to a serving dish. Garnish with fresh thyme leaves if desired. Serve hot with boiled green bananas, dumplings, fried plantains, or rice.

Enjoy the flavors of Jamaica with this delicious and hearty dish of Ackee and Saltfish!

Puerto Rican Pastelón (Plantain Lasagna)

Ingredients:

- 4-5 ripe plantains, peeled and sliced lengthwise
- 1 pound ground beef
- 1 onion, finely chopped
- 2 cloves garlic, minced
- 1 bell pepper, finely chopped
- 1 can (8 oz) tomato sauce
- 1 teaspoon dried oregano
- 1 teaspoon ground cumin
- Salt and pepper to taste
- 2 cups shredded mozzarella or cheddar cheese
- 1/4 cup sliced green olives (optional)
- 1/4 cup raisins (optional)
- Cooking oil for frying

Instructions:

1. Prepare the Plantains: Peel the ripe plantains and slice them lengthwise into thin strips, about 1/4 inch thick. Heat cooking oil in a large skillet over medium heat. Fry the plantain slices in batches until they are golden brown on both sides. Drain them on paper towels and set aside.
2. Cook the Ground Beef: In the same skillet, add the chopped onion, minced garlic, and bell pepper. Sauté until the vegetables are softened and fragrant. Add the ground beef to the skillet and cook until browned, breaking it up with a spoon as it cooks.
3. Season the Beef: Season the ground beef with dried oregano, ground cumin, salt, and pepper. Stir in the tomato sauce and simmer for a few minutes until the flavors meld together. Taste and adjust the seasoning if needed.
4. Assemble the Pastelón: Preheat your oven to 350°F (175°C). In a greased baking dish, layer half of the fried plantain slices on the bottom. Spread half of the cooked ground beef mixture evenly over the plantains. Sprinkle half of the shredded cheese on top. Repeat the layers with the remaining plantains, beef, and cheese.
5. Optional Ingredients: If using, sprinkle the sliced green olives and raisins over the top layer of cheese.

6. Bake: Cover the baking dish with aluminum foil and bake in the preheated oven for 20-25 minutes, or until the cheese is melted and bubbly.
7. Serve: Once baked, remove the Pastelón from the oven and let it cool for a few minutes before slicing. Serve warm and enjoy the delicious layers of sweet plantains, savory beef, and gooey cheese!

Puerto Rican Pastelón is a flavorful and satisfying dish that's sure to be a hit with family and friends. It's a wonderful representation of Puerto Rican cuisine and perfect for any occasion.

Dominican Sancocho

Ingredients:

- 2 pounds chicken pieces (bone-in, skin-on)
- 1 pound beef (such as flank steak or beef stew meat), cut into chunks
- 1 pound pork ribs or pork chops
- 1 pound yuca (cassava), peeled and cut into chunks
- 1 pound ñame (yautía) or malanga, peeled and cut into chunks
- 1 pound batata (sweet potato), peeled and cut into chunks
- 2 ripe plantains, peeled and cut into chunks
- 2 ears of corn, each cut into 3-4 pieces
- 1 large onion, chopped
- 4 cloves garlic, minced
- 1 bell pepper, chopped
- 2 tomatoes, chopped
- 1 bunch cilantro, chopped
- 1 bunch parsley, chopped
- 1 tablespoon dried oregano
- 1 tablespoon ground cumin
- Salt and pepper to taste
- 2 tablespoons cooking oil
- Water
- Lime wedges for serving

Instructions:

1. Prepare the Meats: Season the chicken pieces, beef chunks, and pork ribs (or chops) with salt and pepper.
2. Brown the Meats: In a large pot or Dutch oven, heat the cooking oil over medium-high heat. Brown the seasoned meats on all sides, working in batches if necessary. Remove the browned meats from the pot and set aside.
3. Sauté Aromatics: In the same pot, add the chopped onion, minced garlic, and chopped bell pepper. Sauté until the vegetables are softened and fragrant.
4. Add Tomatoes and Herbs: Stir in the chopped tomatoes, chopped cilantro, chopped parsley, dried oregano, and ground cumin. Cook for a few minutes until the tomatoes start to break down.
5. Return Meats to Pot: Return the browned meats to the pot with the sautéed vegetables and herbs. Add enough water to cover the meats.

6. Simmer: Bring the pot to a boil, then reduce the heat to low and let the stew simmer, partially covered, for about 1 hour, or until the meats are tender.
7. Add Root Vegetables: Add the yuca (cassava), ñame (yautía) or malanga, batata (sweet potato), and chunks of plantain to the pot. Continue to simmer for another 30-45 minutes, or until the root vegetables are tender.
8. Add Corn: Add the pieces of corn to the pot and simmer for an additional 10-15 minutes, or until the corn is cooked through.
9. Adjust Seasoning: Taste the Sancocho and adjust the seasoning with salt and pepper as needed.
10. Serve: Ladle the Dominican Sancocho into bowls, making sure to include a variety of meats and vegetables in each serving. Serve hot with lime wedges on the side.

Enjoy the rich and comforting flavors of Dominican Sancocho, a true taste of Dominican cuisine!

Maldivian Hedhikaa (Short Eats)

Ingredients:

- 1 cup all-purpose flour
- 1/4 teaspoon salt
- Water (as needed to make dough)
- 200g tuna, canned or cooked and shredded
- 1 onion, finely chopped
- 1 green chili, finely chopped
- 2 tablespoons grated coconut
- 1/4 teaspoon turmeric powder
- 1/4 teaspoon chili powder (adjust to taste)
- Salt to taste
- Oil for deep-frying

Instructions:

1. Prepare the Dough:
    - In a mixing bowl, combine the all-purpose flour and salt. Gradually add water, a little at a time, and knead until you have a smooth and elastic dough. Cover the dough and let it rest for about 30 minutes.
2. Prepare the Filling:
    - In another bowl, combine the shredded tuna, chopped onion, chopped green chili, grated coconut, turmeric powder, chili powder, and salt. Mix well to combine all the ingredients.
3. Shape the Bajiya:
    - Divide the rested dough into small balls, about the size of a walnut. Roll out each ball into a thin circle, about 3-4 inches in diameter.
    - Place a spoonful of the tuna filling in the center of each dough circle. Fold the dough over the filling to form a half-moon shape. Press the edges firmly to seal, using a fork to crimp the edges for a decorative finish.
4. Fry the Bajiya:
    - Heat oil in a deep frying pan or pot over medium heat. Once the oil is hot, carefully add the stuffed dough pockets, a few at a time, into the hot oil.
    - Fry the Bajiya until they are golden brown and crispy on both sides, turning them occasionally to ensure even cooking. This usually takes about 3-4 minutes per side.
    - Once cooked, remove the fried Bajiya from the oil using a slotted spoon and drain them on paper towels to remove excess oil.
5. Serve:

- Serve the Maldivian Bajiya hot as a snack or appetizer. They are delicious on their own or served with a dipping sauce of your choice, such as chili sauce or tamarind chutney.

Enjoy these flavorful and crispy Maldivian Bajiya as a delightful snack or appetizer, perfect for any occasion!

Seychellois Ladob (Banana Dessert)

Ingredients:

- 4 ripe bananas, peeled and sliced
- 1 cup coconut milk
- 1/4 cup granulated sugar (adjust to taste)
- 1/2 teaspoon ground cinnamon
- 1/4 teaspoon ground nutmeg
- Pinch of salt
- 1 vanilla pod or 1 teaspoon vanilla extract
- Optional: grated coconut for garnish

Instructions:

1. Prepare the Bananas: Peel the ripe bananas and slice them into rounds, about 1/2 inch thick.
2. Prepare the Coconut Milk Mixture: In a saucepan, combine the coconut milk, granulated sugar, ground cinnamon, ground nutmeg, and a pinch of salt. Split the vanilla pod lengthwise and scrape out the seeds. Add the vanilla seeds (or vanilla extract) to the saucepan. If using a vanilla pod, you can also add the pod itself for additional flavor.
3. Cook the Mixture: Place the saucepan over medium heat and bring the coconut milk mixture to a gentle simmer, stirring occasionally to dissolve the sugar. Let it simmer for a few minutes to allow the flavors to meld together.
4. Add the Bananas: Once the coconut milk mixture is simmering, add the sliced bananas to the saucepan. Gently stir to coat the bananas in the coconut milk mixture.
5. Simmer: Reduce the heat to low and let the bananas simmer gently in the coconut milk mixture, stirring occasionally, until the bananas are tender and the sauce has thickened slightly. This usually takes about 10-15 minutes.
6. Adjust Sweetness: Taste the Ladob and adjust the sweetness if needed by adding more sugar, if desired.
7. Serve: Once the bananas are tender and the sauce has reached the desired consistency, remove the saucepan from the heat. Ladle the Seychellois Ladob into serving bowls or plates.
8. Garnish: If desired, garnish the Ladob with grated coconut for added texture and flavor.
9. Enjoy: Serve the Seychellois Ladob warm as a comforting dessert, either on its own or with a scoop of vanilla ice cream or a dollop of whipped cream on top.

Enjoy this delicious and tropical Seychellois dessert, highlighting the flavors of ripe bananas and creamy coconut milk!

Fijian Rourou (Taro Leaves in Coconut Cream)

Ingredients:

- 1 bunch taro leaves (rourou), washed and chopped
- 1 can (14 oz) coconut milk
- 1 onion, finely chopped
- 2 cloves garlic, minced
- 1-2 chilies, finely chopped (optional)
- Salt to taste
- Cooking oil

Instructions:

1. Prepare the Taro Leaves: Wash the taro leaves thoroughly under cold running water to remove any dirt or debris. Trim off any tough stems and chop the leaves into small pieces.
2. Sauté Aromatics: Heat a little cooking oil in a large saucepan or pot over medium heat. Add the finely chopped onion, minced garlic, and chopped chilies (if using). Sauté until the onions are translucent and fragrant.
3. Add Taro Leaves: Add the chopped taro leaves to the saucepan. Stir well to combine with the sautéed aromatics.
4. Cook the Leaves: Pour the coconut milk over the taro leaves in the saucepan. Stir to combine. Bring the mixture to a gentle simmer.
5. Simmer: Reduce the heat to low and let the taro leaves simmer gently in the coconut milk, stirring occasionally. Cook until the leaves are tender and cooked through, and the coconut milk has thickened slightly. This usually takes about 15-20 minutes.
6. Season: Taste the Fijian Rourou and season with salt to taste. Adjust the seasoning if needed.
7. Serve: Once the taro leaves are tender and the coconut cream has thickened to your liking, remove the saucepan from the heat.
8. Enjoy: Serve the Fijian Rourou hot as a side dish alongside other Fijian dishes, such as fish or meat curries, rice, or roti.

Fijian Rourou is a delicious and comforting dish that highlights the flavors of taro leaves and creamy coconut milk. Enjoy its rich and flavorful taste as part of a Fijian-inspired meal!

www.ingramcontent.com/pod-product-compliance
Lightning Source LLC
LaVergne TN
LVHW061940070526
838199LV00060B/3889